JUDGES
FOR YOU

EDITED FROM THE STUDY BY
TIMOTHY KELLER

JUDGES FOR YOU

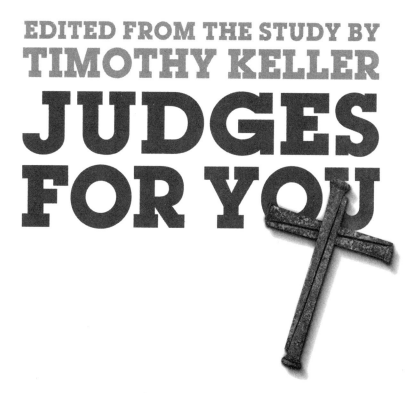

thegoodbook
COMPANY

Judges For You

© Timothy Keller, 2013.
Reprinted 2013, 2014, 2016, 2018, 2019.

Published by:
The Good Book Company

thegoodbook.com | www.thegoodbook.co.uk
thegoodbook.com.au | thegoodbook.co.nz | thegoodbook.co.in

(Hardcover) ISBN: 9781908762900
(Paperback) ISBN: 9781908762863

Printed in India

Design by André Parker

CONTENTS

SERIES PREFACE

Each volume of the *God's Word For You* series takes you to the heart of a book of the Bible, and applies its truths to your heart.

The central aim of each title is to be:

- Bible centered
- Christ glorifying
- Relevantly applied
- Easily readable

You can use *Judges For You:*

To read. You can simply read from cover to cover, as a book that explains and explores the themes, encouragements and challenges of this part of Scripture.

To feed. You can work through this book as part of your own personal regular devotions, or use it alongside a sermon or Bible-study series at your church. Each chapter is divided into two shorter sections, with questions for reflection at the end of each.

To lead. You can use this as a resource to help you teach God's word to others, both in small-group and whole-church settings. You'll find tricky verses or concepts explained using ordinary language, and helpful themes and illustrations along with suggested applications.

This is not a series of commentaries. They assume no understanding of the original Bible languages, nor a high level of biblical knowledge. Verse references are marked in **bold** so that you can identify them easily. Any words that are used rarely or differently in everyday language outside the church are marked in **gray** when they first appear, and are explained in a glossary toward the back. There you'll also find details of resources you can use alongside this one, for both personal and church life.

Our prayer is that as you read, you'll be struck not by the contents of this book, but by the book it's helping you open up; and that you'll praise not the author of this book, but the One he is pointing you to.

Carl Laferton, Series Editor

INTRODUCTION TO JUDGES

"Whatever controls us really is our god … The person who seeks power is controlled by power. The person who seeks acceptance is controlled by the people he or she wants to please. We do not control ourselves. We are controlled by the lord of our life."

(Rebecca Manley Pippert, Out of the Saltshaker, page 48-49)

We live and work among a great variety of gods—not only those of other formal religions, but also the gods of wealth, celebrity, pleasure, ideology, achievement. Our era can be characterized by the phrase which sums up the book of Judges: "Everyone did what was right in his own eyes" (Judges 21:25, ESV).

So despite the gap of over three millennia, there are many parallels between our situation and the time of the book of Judges, which recounts the history of God's people, Israel, between the time of Moses and Joshua, and that of the first kings—around 1200BC. This was a time of spiritual pluralism. The society of Canaan—the land God had promised to give his people, and where they were now living intermingled with other nations—was a mixture of believing and pagan people. It was a time when God's people daily faced the choice between looking to God as their Lord, or following the spirit and preferences of their age. It is mainly the story of how they failed in this task—of how they constantly turned from knowing, loving and obeying God to do "what was right in [their] own eyes."

And so Judges can be described as "despicable people doing deplorable things" and as "trashy tales about dysfunctional characters." As the history unfolds even the "heroes," the judges, become increasingly flawed and failing. They do many appalling things, and their efforts have less and less redemptive effect. It is a dismal story—and it is all history. So the reader will be led to ask, again and again: *What in the world is this doing in the Bible?*

The answer is an important one—it is the gospel! The book of Judges shows us that the Bible is not a "Book of Virtues;" it is not full of inspirational stories. Why? Because the Bible (unlike the books on which other religions are based) is not about following moral examples. It is about a God of mercy and long-suffering, who continually works in and through us despite our constant resistance to his purposes. Ultimately, there is only one hero in this book, and he's divine. When we read this part of Scripture as a historical recounting of how God works to rescue his undeserving people through, and out of, the mess their sin brings them into, then it comes alive to us in our heads and hearts, and speaks into our own lives and situations today. Judges is not an easy read. But living in the times we do, it is an essential one.

> There is only one hero in this book, and he's divine.

So what are the main themes—or, we might say, truths about God—that the writer of Judges wants us to learn and live by? here are six, by way of introduction, to look out for as we go through:

1. *God relentlessly offers his grace to people who do not deserve it, or seek it, or even appreciate it after they have been saved by it.* The book of Judges is not about a series of role models. Though there are a few good examples (eg: Othniel, Deborah), they are early on in the book, and do not dominate the narrative. The point is that the only true savior is the Lord. Judges is ultimately about grace abounding to chief sinners. God's grace will triumph over the stupidest actions.

2. *God wants lordship over every area of our lives, not just some.* God wanted Israel to take the entire land of Canaan, but instead they only cleared out some areas and they learned to live with idols in their midst. In other words, they neither wholly rejected God nor wholly accepted him. This halfway discipleship and

compromise is depicted by the book of Judges as an impossible, unstable compound. God wants all of our lives, not just part.

3. *There is a tension between grace and law, between conditionality and unconditionality.* We find in Judges a seeming contradiction. On the one hand, God demands obedience because he is holy. On the other hand, he makes promises of commitment and loyalty to his people. Will his holiness and his conditional commands (*Do this and then I'll do this*) override his promises (*I will always be with you, no matter what you do*), or will his promises override his commands? Put it this way—are his promises conditional, or unconditional? Judges is crucial, in that it shows that neither answer to that question is right.

Nearly all readers of the Old Testament take a "liberal" view (*Sure, God will always bless us as long as we are sorry*) or a "conservative" view (*No, God will only bless us if we are obedient*). Judges leaves us with a tension—that both are true, but neither are fully true—and it will not resolve the tension. But it is that tension that propels the narrative. Only the New Testament gospel will show us how the two sides can be, and are, both true.

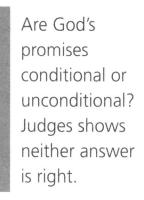

Are God's promises conditional or unconditional? Judges shows neither answer is right.

4. *There is a need for continual spiritual renewal in our lives here on earth, and a way to make that a reality.* Judges shows that spiritual decline is inevitable, and spiritual renewal then becomes the continual need. We will see a regular, repeated decline-revival cycle. Some of the elements in this renewal include repentance, prayer, the destruction of idols, and anointed human leaders. Renewal happens when we are under the right master/ruler; slavery occurs when we are under the wrong master/ruler. Judges is the best book in the Old Testament for the understanding of renewal

and revival, while Acts is the best place in the New Testament. Watch, though, for the way that the revival cycles in Judges become weaker and weaker as time goes on, while in Acts they grow wider and stronger.

5. *We need a true Savior, to which all human saviors point, through both their flaws and strengths.* As we noted above under #1, the increasing magnitude of evil and brokenness in the narrative points us to our need of a savior, not role models. But the decreasing effectiveness of the revival cycles and the decreasing quality of the judges point us to the failure of any human savior. The judges themselves begin to point us to someone beyond them all. In Othniel we learn that God can save through all, in Deborah that he can save through many, in Gideon that he can save through few, and in Samson that he can save through one. God will save by sending the One.

6. *God is in charge, no matter what it looks like.* The most pervasive theme may be the easiest to miss! God often seems almost absent from the scene in Judges, but he never is. He works out his will through weak people, and in spite of weak people. His purposes are never thwarted, regardless of appearances. The mills of God may grind slow, but they grind exceeding fine.

Of course, a book of this length cannot deal fully with every verse of a book of Judges' length. I have interacted with various interpretations of some particularly strange, tricky or controversial passages. One of the biggest problems the modern reader has with Judges (and Joshua) in particular, and the Old Testament in general, is God's order to Israel to "drive out" the inhabitants of Canaan from their homeland; since this is a very difficult issue, and one which underlies the whole book of Judges, I've laid out some thoughts in an appendix, which you'll find on page 211.

As we go through, I'll point at times to the structure both of the book as a whole, and the episodes within it; on pages 207-209, you'll find some resources to help you see the general structure, who the different judges were and how they were similar and different, at a glance; and on page 210, there is a map showing all the places where the key action happens.

But mostly, I've tried to let the narrative speak for itself (the stories, while often depressing and sometimes disturbing, are always exciting and unpredictable); and to draw out the ways we are being pointed to Jesus, the ultimate Judge, and being shown how to live lives which are honoring and pleasing to him among our pluralistic societies today.

1. HALF-HEARTED DISCIPLESHIP

The book of Judges begins by looking backwards, and ends by looking forwards. This period of Israel's history opens: "After the death of **Joshua***" (**1:1**†); its final words strain toward the age of monarchy, of Saul, David, Solomon and their successors: "In those days Israel had no king; everyone did as he saw fit" (21:25). To understand and appreciate the great peaks and troughs, the triumphs and (more often) the tragedies of the time of the judges, we must begin by looking over our shoulders, as **1:1** encourages us to do.

The Promise-Keeping God

Joshua was **Moses**' God-chosen successor to lead the people of Israel (Numbers 27:12-23). He was one of only two men in the whole generation that had been rescued from **Egypt** who had remained faithful in trusting God's promises to bring his people to the promised land of **Canaan** (Numbers 14:30). So he and Caleb (who we meet later in Judges 1) were the only two who escaped God's judgment of death in the desert, and were able to enter the promised land.

The book of Joshua charts God's work in and through his people to keep his promises to them, to bring them into the land, to defeat their enemies, and to begin to give them blessing and rest. It is a book which teaches us that, since God always keeps his promises, God's people can bravely obey and worship him. It is also a book which sets the scene for Judges.

---

* Words in **gray** are defined in the Glossary (page 199).
† All Judges verse references being looked at in each chapter are in **bold**.

At the beginning and end of Joshua, God gives specific directions to Joshua and the people which provide us with a yardstick to measure their progress in Judges 1. First, God tells them the dimensions of the land "I will give you" (Joshua 1:3-4). Second, he reminds them that their LORD-dependent military advances must be accompanied by a close and humble spiritual life—a walk with God. They must "be careful to obey all the law ... meditate on it" (v 7, 8). Victory and rest will come because they are the dependent, obedient people of God; they will not become the people of God through achieving victory and rest for themselves. They are not to expect success if they do not accompany all their work with obedience to God as they **meditate** on his word and trust in his promises.

> Israel will not become God's people by achieving victory for themselves.

The book of Joshua records the beginning of this process of entering and taking the land. For the most part, the people obediently trust God; and God grants them victory. But as Joshua nears the end of his days, there is still much to be done. The land lies open to Israel; but they still need to settle it, trusting God to push out the current inhabitants.

The people still need to trust God to keep his promises, and so bravely obey him: "You will take possession of [this] land, as the LORD your God promised you. Be very strong; be careful to obey all that is written in the **Book of the Law**" (23:5-6).

One outworking of this promise-relying-obedience—what we could call covenant faithfulness—is that Israel must not enter into **covenants** with other nations, serve their gods, or intermarry with them (23:7, 12). The purpose for driving out the Canaanites is not vengeful or economic, but spiritual. They are to be removed so that Israel will not fall under their religious influence—"you are to hold fast to the LORD your God, as you have until now" (v 7). They were to build a home country to serve God in, a land where surrounding nations would be able to see the true God through the lives of his people.

Brave Spirituality

God's call to his people (then and now) is to combine spirituality with bravery. True **discipleship** is radical and risk-taking, because true disciples rely on God to keep his promises to bless them, and not on their own instincts, plans, or insurance policies.

It is hard to be truly *brave* without faith in God. The kind of bravery that does not arise out of faith in God is adventurism, or macho heroism, or plain cruelty. It can be rooted in insecurity, or a desperation to prove oneself, or hopelessness. Only faith-based bravery will walk the line between atrocities on the one side, and cowardice and ineffectiveness on the other.

Faith in God's promises means not always following the expected, rational path. As Joshua dies, it will take real faith to conduct this campaign in the way God wishes. On the one hand, the Israelites can never turn back from fighting any people-group in Canaan, no matter how much stronger they are than Israel. Ordinary military policy dictates that you don't fight superior armies over whom you have no advantage, numerically or technologically. On the other hand, Israel cannot simply plunder and enslave any people-group in Canaan, no matter how much weaker they are than the Israelites. Ordinary military policy dictates that you don't go to the trouble of driving out people who aren't dangerous and who you can dominate and exploit economically. Who Israel chooses to fight, and how Israel responds to victory, will show whether they are truly trusting in the promises—whether they are really obeying the LORD.

Judges, at last!

The opening chapter of Judges, read in light of and measured against the yardstick of the book of Joshua, is a narrative masterpiece. God's verdict on the progress of the Israelites will not (as we'll see) come until the beginning of chapter 2. But the narrative itself shows us that Israel, at this point, is faithful but flawed. The foundations are being laid—and though they are strong in parts, they begin to erode from the outset.

Chapter 1 tracks the successes (and otherwise) of nine of the **tribes of Israel**. Much of the focus falls on Judah, since God says they are to be the first to complete the conquest of their allotted territory (**v 2**).

Almost immediately, Judah fails. "Then the men of Judah said to the Simeonites their brothers, "Come up with us … to fight" (**v 3**). This is common sense, militarily. But it is faithlessness, spiritually. God's word was "Judah is to go"—Judah fails fully to obey. They go, but they do not go alone. Their discipleship is half-way.

Nevertheless, having gone up as directed, "when Judah attacked, the LORD gave the Canaanites and Perizzites into their hands" (**v 4**). They rout the inhabitants, and capture and kill Adoni-Bezek ("the Lord of Bezek"), who recognizes the rightness of this judgment on him ("God has paid me back for what I did to them," **v 7**). It is notable that, while many 21st-century readers have many qualms about Israel's conduct in Canaan, this defeated Canaanite did not. God's judgment throughout history is to give people over to the consequences of the life they have chosen (eg: Psalm 64:3-4, 7-8; Romans 1:21-32)—Adoni-Bezek, it appears, accepts this.

Having won this victory, Judah continues to take their inheritance (**Judges 1:8-11, 17-18**). Between the record of these victories, the narrator narrows the focus to one spiritually brave family in Israel—the family of faithful Caleb. Here, in miniature, is what all Israel should be like. Caleb offers his daughter to a man "who attacks and captures Kiriath Sepher" (**v 12**). What he wants for Acsah is the life he has chosen for himself; one of covenant faithfulness, of courageous obedience in response to God's promises. "Othniel son of Kenaz, Caleb's younger brother, took it" (**v 13**).

> Caleb's family is, in miniature, what all Israel should be like.

Acsah then shows that she is her father's daughter. Her urging of her new husband, Othniel, to ask Caleb for a field (**v 14**), and her own request to Caleb to "give me also springs of water" (**v 15**), displays her desire to take, settle in and enjoy the blessings of the promised land. Caleb, Othniel (who we'll meet again in 3:1-6) and particularly Acsah each show us whole-hearted discipleship. In this sense, they—and the Kenites (**1:16**), distant relatives of Israel who nevertheless "went up ... to live among the people of the Desert of Judah"—stand as a rebuke to the rest of the people. As will often be the case in this book (as well as among God's people today) it is the unlikely and the outsider—a woman and the Kenites—who display real, radical faith.

Common Sense

If chapter 1 finished with **verse 18**, it would be almost completely encouraging, and bode well for the rest of Judges. But **verse 19** jars. "The Lord was with the men of Judah"—and yet "they were unable to drive the people from the plains, because they had iron chariots." Judah does not trust in God's strength, so they measure their own strength against their enemies', and fail to push the chariot-owning plain-dwellers out of the land.

Common, but faithless, sense, begins to prevail here. Judah doesn't trust God; and so they don't secure their inheritance so that they can worship God without compromise. The remaining Canaanites will prove to be a thorn in their side for centuries to come.

It is not our lack of strength that prevents us from enjoying God's blessings, or from worshiping God wholeheartedly; it is our lack of faith in *his* strength. When we rely on ourselves, and base our walk with God on our own calculations instead of simply obeying, we find ourselves making decisions like the Judaites. Othniel attacked a city in God's strength; the tribe of Judah concluded they could not do likewise in their own. It is halfway discipleship, and Judges will show us that it leads to no discipleship at all. The warning to us is clear!

Nor, Neither, Nor

The contagion of half-hearted obedience, of half-belief in God's promises, spreads. The tribe of Benjamin fails "to dislodge the Jebusites" (**v 21**). The house of Joseph makes covenants with a Canaanite, instead of trusting God's covenant promises (**v 22-26**). Manasseh fails to drive out various inhabitants, and then when they are strong enough, decides to exploit them as forced labor (**v 27-28**). The reason implied is that it made more economic sense and required less effort to enslave them than to drive them out. Convenience trumps obedience.

Ephraim allows Canaanites to live among them (**v 29**). Zebulun opts for forced labor (v 30). The people of Asher fare still worse; instead of allowing Canaanites to live among them, they live among Canaanites (**v 31-32**), as does Naphtali (**v 33**). Lastly, the tribe of Dan become "confined … to the hill country" (**v 34**). What matters in **verse 36** is not the borders of the allotted inheritance of Israel, but the border of the Amorites, the areas where they "were determined … to hold out" (**v 35**). Here, there is no claim of greater military resources or numbers. Rather, the reason given is superior will-power and tenacity—superior courage. God's people have become less brave than the people who do not know him.

In many ways, and at first reading, this is a chapter of great conquest. Israel lives in the promised land, and has settled great areas of it. Two generations previously, as the Israelites suffered under the yoke of slavery in Egypt, they could not have dreamed that this would be the lives their grandchildren lived. But—and it is a big "but"—Israel has not fully trusted or obeyed. And the Israelites now live alongside **idol**-worshiping Canaanites. Like buried mines, these idols lie dormant in Judges 1, ready to explode in the spiritual lives of God's people.

Questions for reflection

1. Can you think of times in your life when you have been brave because of your faith?

2. When do you find it hardest to follow God's commands instead of your own "common sense." Why?

3. Think of areas of your life where you are enjoying "success." Are you still radically relying on God and obeying him in those areas?

PART TWO

God Speaks

When read through the lens of the book of Joshua, we can see the halfway discipleship on display in Judges 1. But when read in isolation, there do seem to be very plausible reasons for why the Israelites did not succeed in their campaign—inferior military might, sensible compromise, economic convenience. How could they drive out iron chariots when they had none (**1:19**)?

Taken on its own terms, chapter 1 reads a little like a collection of Israel's press releases about their campaign. It's their "spin" on why they weren't as successful as we (and God) might have expected. The readers are lulled into sympathy with the Israelites. When we are told that they "could not drive out" (**v 19**, ESV) the Canaanites, we are inclined to agree. They did their best.

Then suddenly we are confronted and shocked by God's assessment. Chapter 1 has given us the facts. Now we have heaven's explanation, as "the angel of the LORD went up from Gilgal to Bokim and said…" (**2:1**). The Bible narratives are often structured like this. At the beginning of Jesus' life, the bare details of his birth in Bethlehem (Luke 2:4-7) are followed by the angel's explanation of their significance (2:8-14). At the other end of his earthly ministry, the women are confronted by the cold reality of the empty tomb (Mark 16:4), and then what their eyes are seeing is explained by two heavenly messengers— the tomb is empty because "he has risen! He is not here" (v 5-7).

The route the angel takes is important. Why does he go "up from Gilgal," a town to the west of the River Jordan, close to the city of Jericho (Judges **2:1**)? Surely the angel of the LORD does not live in Gilgal?! Why the reference? Because it was in Gilgal in Joshua 5 that the people made a covenant with God, and where he said: "Today I have rolled away the reproach of Egypt from you" (Joshua 5:9—"Gilgal" means "to roll"). This was the place where God had forgiven their sin, bound them to himself as his people, and entered into relationship with them by grace, motivated only by his own loving kindness.

So when the angel comes from Gilgal, it is a reminder to the Israelites that they are saved by **grace**. It is a reminder that, as the angel says in Judges **2:1**, the LORD is a rescuing, promise-keeping, faithful God.

You Have Disobeyed

The God of grace's assessment of his people's performance is scathing. "You have disobeyed me" (**v 2**). Period.

How has Israel disobeyed God? Through what they have done: they made "a covenant with the people of this land," despite being told "you shall not." And through what they have not done: they have failed to "break down their **altars**" (**v 2**). This is the purpose of the campaign. This military campaign is not an ethnic cleansing—Rahab the Canaanite prostitute was allowed to stay (Joshua 2:17-20, 6:25); the Kenites settled with Judah (Judges **1:16**). And the campaign is not an imperialistic conquest, since no one is allowed to take plunder or slaves. The purpose is to cleanse Canaan from idols, so that Israel is able to live in covenant faithfulness to the LORD. By allowing the Canaanites to continue to live in the land, or by making covenant agreements with them—for whatever reason—the end result is that idols are being worshiped in the midst of the Israelites.

The basic teaching is that God wants lordship over every area of our lives, not just some of them. God wanted Israel to clear the whole of Canaan so that his people would not end up living with idols as well as with him. That they did not reveals that, though they had not wholly rejected God as their God, they had not wholly accepted him, either. This halfway discipleship and compromise is depicted throughout Judges as an unstable compound. It cannot last. Ultimately, either

Halfway discipleship is an unstable compound. It cannot last.

all of our life is given to God in grateful, loving obedience; or none is. Part-obedience, as we'll see, tends toward non-obedience.

Can't, or Won't?

In **1:19**, we read the Israelites "were unable." **2:2** is a flat contradiction of this claim. Essentially, the Israelites said: *We could not.* And God answers here: *You would not.*

It is worth asking ourselves: *Where am I saying "I can't" but God is saying "You won't"?* Israel's failure to obey was based on what they saw as good reasons—God said they were flimsy excuses. Why? Because "God is faithful; he will not let you be tempted beyond what you can bear" (1 Corinthians 10:13). God will never put us in a position where we cannot obey him. There is never a real "I can't" moment.

So these verses are very searching and challenging to apply to ourselves. There may be all sorts of things in our lives which we think we are unable to do, but which actually we are refusing to do. Much of the book of Judges shows how God is faithful to us despite our disobedience—that is comforting. But Judges also shows us that God in his grace will insist on removing our self-deception about our motives and actions.

There are three general categories of "can't" justifications for disobedience:

1. Forgiveness: *I can't forgive this, or him, or her.* But God commands forgiveness (Matthew 18:35). So we can, in fact, determine to put aside anger and soften our hearts with the knowledge of the **gospel** of grace, and act as though the wrong had not happened. When we say we can't, we mean we won't; that we want to hang on to our anger, our bitterness, our "right" to get even, under the excuse of being "unable."

2. Difficult truth-telling: *I just can't tell him the truth. It would destroy him/me.* God tells us to "speak the truth in love" (Ephesians

4:15, 25). Often, we are excusing cowardice or pride under "can't." What we really mean is: *If I tell him that, he may not like me anymore. I would be humiliated. He would be upset. I won't risk that cost— I would rather disobey.*

3. Temptation: *I can't resist doing this, though I know it is wrong.* We must be careful here, because sin has addictive power—it is true that we may not be able, through sheer willpower, to stop doing something by ourselves. But we can get help, admit our problem, humble ourselves, cry out to God for mercy and transformation, become accountable. God always gives us a way out (1 Corinthians 10:13)—no sinful thought or action is inevitable and irresistible. If we don't, it's likely that we would simply rather keep sinning in that way, excusing it with our "inability" to do anything else.

How do we treat our won'ts? God sees that any failure to obey is a failure to *remember*. God is the God who rescues—"I brought you up out of Egypt" (Judges **2:1**); and God is the God who remains faithful—"I will never break my covenant with you." The root of our disobedience is essentially failing to remember who he is. And the reverse is true—for as long as we remember who he is, we will serve him wholeheartedly, radically, *and* joyfully.

> As long as we remember who God is, we will serve him radically *and* joyfully.

The Israelites had failed to do this. And the consequences were clear, and catastrophic. "Therefore"—because of your covenant-breaking disobedience—"I tell you that I will not drive them out before you; they will be thorns in your sides and their gods will be a snare to you" (**v 3**).

This is a very illuminating description of what **idolatry** is, and does. Idolatry is making a good aspect of creation—marriage, mountains, business, and so on—into the ultimate source of security, identity, and power. And so false gods are a thorn. When we make something into an idol, it continually makes us miserable. If we fall short of it, or if we might fall short of it, it robs us of joy. If our children are our false god, when their lives are troubled, we will lose our joy; and even when their lives *might* become troubled (which is all the time!), we will worry, and lose our joy.

And idols are **snares**. They trap us. When we make something into an idol, it binds and enslaves us. We *have* to have it, so we cannot say *no* to it. We are addicted to it. This is why many people work too hard, sacrificing family, friendships and health at the altar of career; or give themselves to certain relationships that are destructive; and so on.

In Judges 2, the people respond by weeping (**v 4**) and offering **sacrifices** (**v 5**). This first post-Joshua generation have not fully turned away from the Lord, though they have failed to obey him fully. They are truly half-hearted disciples—and this leaves them and (as we'll see) their children surrounded by thorns and snares, by the constant temptation to compromise in their love for and obedience to the rescuing, faithful God. The scene is set for the book of Judges—the people of God seeking, and more often failing, to live **holy** lives which please him, in the middle of an idolatrous culture.

The Tension of Judges

There is a tension between God's "I said" in **verse 1**, and his "I tell you" in **verse 3**. This tension is stronger than most English translations indicate, as Michael Wilcock explains:

> "2:1 and 2:3 should be read like this: 'I said, I will never break my covenant … and I also said, If you compromise with these nations I will not drive them out'. It is as though the Lord is saying, 'I have sworn to give you the whole of this land, yet I have also sworn not to give it to a disobedient people.'"
>
> (*The Message of Judges*, page 27)

This is how we should understand the end of **verse 2**: "Why have you done this?" God is saying to his people: *You have put me in an impossible situation. I have sworn to bless you as my beloved people, and sworn not to bless you as disobedient people. How am I to solve this dilemma?*

On the one hand, God is holy and just and cannot tolerate or live with or bless evil. On the other hand, God is loving and faithful and cannot tolerate the loss of people he has committed himself to. This is a tremendous, seemingly irresolvable tension in the narrative—and also in the whole Bible (see, for instance, Exodus 34:6-7; Hosea 11:1-11). This tension is what should keep us in suspense throughout Judges. Will God finally give up on his people (but then what of his faithfulness)? Or will he finally give in to his people (but then what of his holiness)?

It is only on the cross that we can understand how God is able to resolve the tension. On the cross, our sin was given—**imputed**—to him, so that his righteousness could be imputed to us. On the cross, "God made him who had no sin to be sin for us, so that in him we might become the righteousness of God" (2 Corinthians 5:21). On the cross, God poured out his **wrath** on his people in the person of his Son. He satisfied both justice, because sin was punished, and loving faithfulness, since he is now able to accept and forgive us. Only through the cross can God be both "just and the justifier of the one who has faith in Jesus" (Romans 3:26, ESV). This is the only way the tension of Judges can be resolved; the only way that God can love us both conditionally *and* unconditionally.

Without the gospel of Christ crucified, we will always either complacently give in to sin (because of the unconditionality of his promises), or live under a burden of guilt and fear (because of their conditionality). The cross is where we find the tension resolved, so we are

> Without the gospel, we will always be complacent or burdened.

able to live forgiven, obedient lives despite also living sinful, disobedient lives. The cross is the place where we find the freedom to accept ourselves without being proud, and to challenge ourselves without being crushed.

Questions for reflection

1. In which parts of your life and thinking do you most need to be reminded today that God is a God of *grace*?

2. Where are you saying to God: *I cannot*? Do you need to accept that in fact you are saying: *I will not*? How will you change?

3. How will the cross motivate you to make these changes?

2. LIVING AMONG IDOLS

Chapter 2:6 – 3:6 is a second introduction to the book of Judges, which is best read parallel to 1:1 – 2:5. But it is not only an introduction: it is a summary of the whole book. In it, the narrator lays out the cycle of Israelite spiritual experience which we will see repeated through the book. And, while 2:4-5 offered some hope for Israel's future, as the half-hearted people wept at their disobedience and offered sacrifices to God, this second introduction, by taking us further in time, ends on a much more depressing note about the spiritual state of God's people (3:5-6).

A Life Well Lived

The second introduction, like the first one, begins with Joshua, the great yardstick for the book of Judges. Having "dismissed the Israelites ... to take possession of the land" (**v 6**), "the people served the LORD" throughout the lifetimes of Joshua and his lieutenants. This was a generation who "had seen all the great things the LORD had done for Israel" (**v 7**) as he brought them into the land and defeated their enemies.

Joshua's was a life well lived. He was supremely a "servant of the LORD" (**v 8**). And, unlike every leader of Israel from **Joseph** to Moses, he had the privilege of dying and being buried "in the land of his inheritance" (**v 9**).

But there is something troubling in these verses. Chapter 1 has already shown that the settling of the Israelite tribes, and their service of the LORD, was done half-heartedly and incompletely. Joshua himself had warned these people: "You are not able to serve the LORD ... If you forsake the LORD and serve foreign gods, he will turn and bring disaster on you ... throw away the foreign gods that are among you and yield your hearts to the LORD, the God of Israel" (Joshua 24:19-20, 23).

If this imperfect, flawed generation, clearly already struggling with "foreign gods that are among you" and "not able to serve the LORD," can be described in positive terms in Judges **2:6-9**, it begs the question: *What would a truly idolatrous generation look like?* The answer is not long in coming...

Another Generation

Verses 10-11 describe a rebellion. It had two stages. First, the generation after Joshua's "knew neither the LORD nor what he had done for Israel" (**v 10**). The word "knew" probably does not mean that they did not know *about* the **Exodus**, the **Red Sea**, the **crossing of the Jordan**, and the **walls of Jericho** falling, but rather that the saving acts of God were no longer precious or central to them. They had not learned to revere and rejoice in what God had done. In other words, they had forgotten the "gospel" that they were saved from slavery in Egypt and brought into the promised land by the gracious, mighty acts of God. Put simply, they *forgot*.

Second, and as a result of forgetting the gospel, they "did evil in the eyes of the LORD and served the Baals" (**v 11**). This is an interesting parallel. What does God say is evil? Turning to love and serve idols, mini-gods, non-gods. This is a very different definition of "doing evil" than the one we usually use! It is also much more challenging to us.

The word "Baal" is a Canaanite word for "lord." This new generation forget all about the LORD and instead serve mini-lords.

It is striking that this happens within a generation. Their parents, though flawed and sometimes half-hearted, had faith—they "served the LORD." The children "served the mini-lords." Who is responsible?

It is always impossible to lay blame neatly when one generation fails to pass its faith on to the next one. Did the first generation fail to reach out, or did the second generation just harden their hearts? The answer is usually both. Mistakes made by a Christian generation are often magnified in the next, **nominal**, one. Commitment is replaced by complacency and then by compromise.

Judges 2 is by no means the last or only time this has happened. Another interesting example is early New England. Nearly all the first settlers in 1620–1640 were vital, biblical Christians. But by 1662, the first generation realized that many of their children and grand-children were only nominal believers. They had to institute the "halfway Covenant," allowing people to vote who were only baptized as infants, but who as adults were not church members.

Deuteronomy 6:4-9 and 20-25 are instructive here. They tell us what needs to be done to pass our faith on:

- We ourselves must love God whole-heartedly. We are to have these commandments on our hearts (v 6). That means that we are not hypocritical or inconsistent in our behavior. The commandments are not only kept mechanically or partially. Rather, God has an effect on all of us, through and through. Younger people are sensitive to any inconsistency. That is the first reason that a younger generation can turn from the faith of an older one. One example is how "**Baby Boomer**" youth turned away from mainstream Christianity when they saw how the churches tacitly or even actively supported racist policies and practices, and when they saw many established churches opposing the **Civil Rights movement**.

- We are to apply and reflect on the gospel practically, not only academically or abstractly. Deuteronomy 6:7 is not promoting regular family lectures! The references to "sit … walk along … lie down and … get up" refer to routine, concrete daily life. Instruction in God's truth then is not to be so much a series of lectures and classes. Rather, we are to "impress" truths about God by showing how God relates to daily, concrete living. This is a call to be wise and thoughtful about how the values and virtues of the gospel distinctively influence our decisions and priorities.

■ Third, verses 20-25 tell us that we are to link the **doctrines** of the faith to God's saving actions in our lives. We are to give personal testimony to the difference God made to us, how he brought us from bondage into freedom: "We were slaves … but the Lord brought us out." We are not only to speak of beliefs and behavior but of our personal experience of God. We are to be open about our own struggles to grow. We are to be transparent about how **repentance** works in our lives. We are not to be formal and impersonal in the expressions of our faith.

In summary, we must be consistent in behavior, wise about reality, and warmly personal in our faith. History and personal experience both show us that these three things are very hard to carry out on a broad scale. Most Christians rely on institutions and formal instruction to "pass on the faith." We think that if we instruct our children in true doctrine, shelter them from immoral behavior and involve them in church and religious organizations, then we have done all we can. But youth are turned off not only by bad examples, but also by parents who are not savvy about the lives and world their children are living in, or who cannot be open about their own interior spiritual lives.

> We must be consistent in behavior, wise about reality, and warmly personal in our faith.

In Judges 2, we are not told exactly what the first generation of believers did with their children. **2:10** is key, however. The next generation did not know the Lord, relationally and personally. This is the very outcome that Deuteronomy 6 was written to avoid. Deuteronomy 6 is not a "technique" that guarantees that someone's children will be believers, because their own wills and choices play a large role.

However, when a whole generation turns away, we have to expect that the parents have failed to model real faith and disciple their children.

The Repeated Cycle

Judges **2:10-13** are the first stage in the cycle that repeats itself in Israel's history throughout Judges, in the time between Joshua's death and God giving his people a king. **The people rebel**. They forsake the Lord, the God their fathers had worshiped and who had rescued them as he had promised; and they decide to become like the people who did not know anything of the Lord, and to worship their gods (**v 12**).

How would God respond? "They provoked the Lord to *anger* … In his *anger* against Israel…" (**v 12, 14**). **God is angry** when people in his world set other things in his place. His anger is not against a particular people group or type (here, he is angry with his own people). Anger is not always the opposite of love; it can be the outworking of it. God here is like a parent whose child has completely rejected them.

So, as a result of Israel's rebellion and God's anger, there is **oppression by enemies**: "The Lord handed them over to raiders who plundered them" (**v 14**). Various people groups rose up or invaded and either plundered or enslaved the Israelites, and "they were no longer able to resist" (**v 14**), because "the hand of the Lord was against them to defeat them" (**v 15**). Don't miss the irony here: these enemies are the very people whose gods Israel has chosen to serve. If there were ever a historical picture of the truth that idolatry leads to slavery, this is it.

Next follows **repentance**. "They were in great distress" (**v 15**). As we'll see, this distress caused the people to cry out to the Lord (3:9). And so finally, God "raised up judges, who saved them" (**2:16**). The Lord sent his **salvation through a chosen leader**, who liberated the people from their slave-masters and returned the land to **peace** (**v 18**). But the judge's leadership was not heeded in any kind of lasting way—"they quickly turned from … the way of obedience" (**v 17**). And, as we'll see, this cycle was in fact a downward spiral—"when **the judge died**, the people returned to ways even more corrupt than those of their fathers" (**v 19**). The thorns dug deeper and deeper; the snares pulled Israel more and more tightly. We will see as Judges progresses that the rebellion becomes worse, the oppression heavier, the repentance less heartfelt, the judges themselves more flawed, and the salvation and "revivals" they bring weaker.

It is a reminder, of course, that we need something better than a human judge; something more permanent than a leader who dies; something that can deliver the soul, as well as the body. We will not find such a rescuer in the book of Judges!

Questions for reflection

1. What would be your spiritual epitaph? In what ways are you living out your calling to be a "servant of the LORD"?

2. *If you are a parent:* How are you passing your faith on to your children? What has encouraged you and what has challenged you today? *If you're not a parent with children living at home:* How are you praying for and sharing your faith with younger generations in your church?

3. How have you seen the "Judges cycle" in your own Christian life? How does the reality of your sin and of God's grace prompt you to praise and thank him today?

PART TWO

It is well worth spending some more time in **verses 16-19**, since they teach us so much about the nature of idolatry.

Married Prostitute

What are God's people doing when they do not listen to their God-given leader (for them then, the judges; for us today, the ultimate leader, Jesus Christ)? What are we doing when we worship other gods instead of the true God? We have "prostituted" ourselves (**v 17**).

This is a striking, provocative image. Prostitutes then (and often now, too) are people whose lives are out of control, who are desperate, and who are giving themselves without getting any real pleasure or love in return. The use of the word "prostituted" here tells us that when we serve an idol, we come into an intense relationship with it, within which it uses us, but does not truly care for us. We become completely vulnerable to it, little more than a slave to it.

This image also tells us that God sees *all* sin—all idolatry—as "adultery." He does not merely want us to know and obey him as a citizen obeys a king, or merely to follow him as a sheep follows a shepherd. He wants us to know him and love him as a wife loves a husband. In both the Old and New Testaments, God calls himself our Bridegroom (Ezekiel 16; Ephesians 5; Revelation 19). A marriage is an exclusive, legal commitment, but it is not *only* that; real marriage involves deep, intimate, selfless love.

Israel, then, was a married prostitute. This is how God pictures his people in one of the most startling passages in the Scriptures, Hosea 1 – 3. God wants Israel to "remove the adulterous look from her face and the unfaithfulness from between her breasts" (2:2)—"she burned incense to the Baals; she decked herself with rings and jewelry, and went after her lovers, but me she forgot, declares the LORD" (v 13). And he tells his prophet, Hosea, to marry a prostitute, Gomer, so that their marriage can serve as a picture of what God will do for his people, and how they will respond: "The LORD said to me: 'Go, show your love to your wife again, though she is loved by another and is an adulteress. Love her as the LORD loves the Israelites' ... So I bought her [Gomer had clearly sold herself into slave-prostitution] ... I told her 'You are to live with me many days; you must not be a prostitute or be intimate with any man, and I will live with you'" (3:1-3).

This shows us why God responds to his people "following other gods and serving and worshiping them" (Judges **2:19**) by becoming "very angry with Israel" (**2:20**). His anger is not opposed to his love; it is the expression of it. It is because he loves his people, and cares about his relationship with them, that he responds with right anger when they turn from him and prostitute themselves. His anger is that of the innocent, jilted lover; his love is that of the wonderfully forgiving husband. The relationship God wants us to enjoy with him—and the only relationship which will avoid idolatry—is a passionate, personal relationship of love.

The Judge or the Idols?

For Israel, the opposite to prostituting themselves to other gods—the way to express love for God—was to "listen to their judges" (**v 17**). Essentially, in each area of their lives, and throughout their lives, every Israelite had to choose whether to follow, serve and obey the gods of the nations around them, or the judge God had sent. They had to choose where to look for salvation—to the judge God raised up to save them (**v 18**), or a false god (see 10:14).

In this sense, the false gods and the God-sent judges are like each other. Both offer to be ruler-saviors.

But they were unlike each other in that the salvation of the judges was by the sheer grace and compassion of God—he "had compassion on them as they groaned" (**2:18**). Groaning is hardly a way of earning your salvation! God sends the salvation simply because the people's hearts are breaking, and because he cares about that. Despite their unfaithfulness to him, he saves them. But there is no indication anywhere of the Canaanite gods "having compassion." False gods can make people into servants (**v 19**) who are deeply, stubbornly enslaved. But false gods cannot show grace, or forgive. They promise much; but they deliver nothing.

Gods, Plural

One of the beauties of Judges is the subtlety of the narrative. So in **verse 19**, we see not that Israel decided to serve one other god—totally swapping the true God for an alternative—but that they were "following other gods." They decided to be unfaithful to the Lord to serve "Baal *and* the Ashtoreths" (**v 13**). The teaching is that it is possible (perhaps even natural) for humans to worship many gods at the same time.

Israel's spiritual life, then, was more complex than a simple decision to stop worshiping the Lord, and start worshiping a different god. In fact, what the Israelites did was to combine the worship of the Lord with idols. As we will see in Judges 17, an Israelite woman gives her valuables to her son, and says: "I solemnly consecrate my silver to the Lord for my son to make a carved image and a cast idol" (17:3).

The **pagan** world-view was that there were many gods (eg: of agriculture, business, love, music, war), each of whom had a particular area of influence, and none of whom demanded lordship over every single area of life. In this view, everyone had his or her own god(s), chosen or discarded on the basis of one's interests and needs. It was a "mix and match" religion in which the worshipper appeared **sovereign**.

Paganism therefore could accept the existence, but not the exclusive sovereignty, of the Lord. He could be one of many. He could even be first among equals. But he could not claim that he was the one true God; that his worshipers give him absolute lordship over every square inch of their lives; that ever to worship another god was spiritual prostitution.

It was this belief system which had led to Israel's failure to take all of Canaan; it was this belief system which the ongoing co-existence of the Canaanites encouraged and facilitated. The promised land was meant to be a place of worship of the LORD alone; it became the land of worship of the LORD plus.

The people's failure to take all of Canaan both resulted from and represented their failure to give God exclusive lordship over their whole lives. It is not hard to see how this might happen today, as we believers live in a pagan world that offers us a vast array of alternative "gods." The greatest danger, because it is such a subtle temptation which enables us to continue as church members and feel that nothing is wrong, is not that we become atheists, but that we ask God to co-exist with idols in our hearts.

> The greatest danger is not atheism, but that we ask God to co-exist with idols.

How can we know if Christ is Lord of every area of our lives? First, we need to identify the false gods of the society around us. For Christians in the west, a statue which promises us fertility is unlikely to attract us. But if a believer lives in a city where commerce is not just a practice but a **functional** god—providing people with identity and security—the danger is that the Christian maintains his or her doctrinal beliefs and **ethical** practices, but divides heart worship between the Lord and money/career.

Second, we need to look honestly at each area of our lives—our families, our careers, our possessions, our ambitions, our time, and so on—and ask two questions of them:

- Am I willing to do whatever God *says* about this area?

- Am I willing to accept whatever God *sends* in this area?

Where either answer is "no," there is the area of our lives and hearts which we have opened up, or already given over, to an alternative god.

The Mercy of Judgment

God's judgment on his people's half-heartedness, and idol-heartedness, is that: "I will no longer drive out before them any of the nations Joshua left when he died" (**2:21**). The job will remain half-finished.

But though God does not drive the Canaanites out, he now uses their presence to accomplish two things for Israel. First, "I will use them to test Israel and see whether they will keep the way of the LORD" (**v 22**). Tests can be failed; but tests can also be passed! A test forces us to learn and study and become disciplined and rise up to meet it. The presence of an enemy which stood opposed to God and his people forced Israel to think about their relationship to God; their own failures; the wisdom of his ways; the distinctiveness he calls his people to.

Second, the narrator lists "the nations the LORD left ... he did this only to teach warfare to the descendants of the Israelites who had not had previous battle experience" (**3:1-2**). Why?

"In the hope that this will develop their dependence upon him in every situation of need."

(David Jackman, *Judges, Ruth,* page 61)

As they entered the promised land under Joshua, the people had learned to trust God to keep his promises, to fight relying on him. Nowhere was this better illustrated than at Jericho, where God told his people to march, but not to fight; and then granted them victory (Joshua 6). This was the lesson Israel had forgotten by the time of Judges 1. God's mercy was to use the nations around Israel to bring them moments when all seemed lost, and so to drive them into greater dependence on him. Surrounded by idol-worshiping peoples, Israel would face the constant question: *Will you obey the LORD's commands* (**3:4**)?

> God's mercy was to use the nations to drive Israel into dependence on him.

Tragically, Israel failed to learn the lesson or to pass the test. They lived among the other nations (**v 5**); and they became like the other nations (**v 6**). They gave in to their sinful desires, and lived lives indistinguishable from the pagans around them, doing evil and glorifying idols. The challenge to us as God's people today is to do the opposite: to recognize that we are "aliens and strangers in the world," and so to "abstain from sinful desires" and "live such good lives among the pagans that ... they may see your good deeds and glorify God" (1 Peter 2:11-12).

Questions for reflection

1. How does the description of sin as spiritual prostitution make you take your own sin more seriously?

2. Look back to the questions on page 38. Which aspects of your life do you struggle to answer "yes" about?

3. Do you see living among non-believers as a problem, a possibility, or both? How can you live a good life among non-believers today?

3. OTHNIEL AND EHUD: EXPECT THE UNEXPECTED

In the long double-introduction, the author, in showing that Israel failed to drive idols out of their land, highlights the dramatic "tension" between God's holy commands, and his loving, faithful promise. God demands obedience, yet he has promised to save his people. As a result of this "tension," the children of Israel go into a cyclical pattern of decline, caused by their idolatry, and revival, brought by God's saving mercy. God continually **chastens** them for their sin, but he then delivers them from their peril. He never casts them off, but continues graciously and severely to work for their growth.

In chapter 3, we now get specific "case histories" which reveal these principles. We meet the first three judges: Othniel, Ehud, and (in one verse!) Shamgar.

Heart-Forgetfulness

"The Israelites did evil in the eyes of the LORD" (**v 7**). As we have already seen, what God calls evil is a twofold decision: to turn away from him, or to "forget" him; and to serve mini-lords, false gods—here, the Baals and the Asherahs (Asherah was a female fertility-goddess).

In the Bible, "remembering" and "forgetting" have a spiritual significance. When people in the Old Testament asked God to "remember … your great mercy and love" (Psalm 25:6) or to "not remember our sins" (Isaiah 64:9), they did not believe that God could literally forget what he is like, or what someone has done! What does it mean, then, to "forget" or "remember"? When God is asked: "Remember your great mercy and love," he is being asked to act according to his character. When someone asks God to "remember not [my] sins," he or she is asking that God would not act on what he knows.

Therefore, to say that the Israelites "forgot" God is to say that they no longer were controlled by what they knew. We could put it another way. Though they knew who God was and what he wanted, those things were not real to them. This is a spiritual problem today, too. What we know with our heads is not "real" to our hearts and our whole beings. We may acknowledge intellectually that something is true, but in our heart of hearts it does not grab us or penetrate us or control us. So, the reason that the Israelites (like all of us) continually needed revival was because truths about God which were once vibrant and real to them eventually became unreal. Our hearts are like a bucket of water on a very cold day—they will freeze over unless we regularly smash the ice that is forming. Though we know truths about God, we can very easily lose the sense upon our hearts of their reality. We know them, but we don't "taste" or "see" or "feel" them. Therefore, other things—idols—become more real to our hearts, and we serve them instead.

The remedy is to reverse our heart-forgetting—in other words, to remember. 2 Peter 1:5-7 urges Christians to grow in their character: in kindness, self-control and so on. But what if they do not? Peter does not say: *Your problem is that you're not trying hard enough*. He says: "If anyone does not have [these qualities], he … has forgotten that he has been cleansed from his past sins" (v 9). And so: "I will always remind you of these things, even though you know them" (v 12). Peter is saying that, if the forgiveness and salvation of Christ is real to you, you will live it out in your character and life. You need to be reminded of what you already

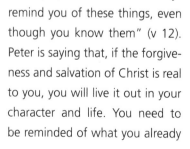

> If forgiveness and salvation is real to you, you will live it out in your life.

know; you need these truths to work in your heart as well as being understood in your head. The problem the Israelites had, we still have, even those of us who believe in Christ and have the Holy Spirit.

How can we make sure we remember? There are many answers. Here are just three suggestions.

- Jesus has given us a visual image of what he has done for us—the Lord's Supper. When he says: "Do this in remembrance of me" (Luke 22:19), he is telling us that this picture-meal is his way of continually renewing the reality of the gospel in our heart.

- Whenever we read the Bible, we should not only study it for content, but we should learn to meditate and reflect on it so that we don't only acknowledge the truths, but we "remember" them and sense them and are moved by them.

- Jesus intended the Lord's Supper to be a community event. We need to be reminded of and study and apply God's truths in groups. When several people look at a truth, one person (at least) is usually able to say *Wow!* The sense that person has of the truth can then spread to those of us who are stagnant or dry.

How God Brings Revival

Judges **3:7** focuses on what the Israelites are doing—forgetting the LORD and worshiping idols. From **verse 8** onwards, God is the main director. His "anger ... burned against Israel" (**v 8**)—so he sends trouble! "he sold them into the hands of Cushan-Rishathaim," just as the people had already sold themselves into the hands of the Baals and Asherahs. Even in judging his people, God is acting kindly. If he had not brought about suffering and difficulty, the people would not have seen their true position. They would not have seen how spiritually enslaved they were, and what a judgment they were facing, if God had not let them taste that judgment by allowing them to become physically enslaved. He sends the Israelites suffering not simply to pay them back, but to redeem them—he still does this for his people (1 Corinthians 11:32).

And, struggling under physical oppression, they finally (after eight years, it appears, Judges **3:8**!) "cried out to the LORD" and "he raised up for them a deliverer" (**v 9**). The only thing the people contribute to their rescue is to cry out to God. This implies that they reversed their previous allegiance, turning away from the idols and back to the LORD as their God—they repented. Repentance is crucial for renewal and restoration. The people did not wait for trouble to go away. They may have asked themselves: *Why has this trouble come? What flaws in us might God be revealing, and how might we need spiritual renewal?* This is the right response to oppression: to see how God's hand is working behind and through it, and look honestly at ourselves, and to cry out to the LORD for revival.

> Repentance is crucial for renewal and restoration.

Having sent trouble, God sends spiritual leadership. His chosen leader is Othniel, the whole-hearted disciple whom we met back in 1:13; the kind of leader we would expect God to choose for his people. This first "judge cycle" is the ideal, and is the only one which fully contains each "stage" which was laid out in 2:11-19. Apart from Joshua, Othniel is the only man throughout Judges whose life is recounted in any detail who isn't explicitly flawed. Literally, the end of **3:9** reads: "he saved them." Who "he" refers to—God, or Othniel—is left unclear, reminding us that God saves his people through his chosen leader, and that both can be said to bring the salvation.

As well as trouble and spiritual leadership, God sends his Spirit (**v 10**). He empowers Othniel for his status and work—the Spirit was sent "so that he became Israel's judge and went to war." (It is interesting to note a significant difference between Old Testament revivals and the New Testament revivals in the book of Acts. Here, as throughout the Old Testament, God sends his Spirit to one leader; in the New

Testament, God sends his Spirit to the whole people, the church—compare **verse 10** with Acts 4:31).

So, in summary, God sends trouble, leadership, and the Spirit of God. And this brings restoration—"The LORD gave Cushan-Rishathaim king of Aram into the hands of Othniel, who overpowered him" (**Judges 3:10**). And this results in spiritual renewal—"the land had peace for forty years" (**v 11**). This is peace from physical oppression, but also from the self-inflicted spiritual oppression of idolatry, which had caused the physical oppression in the first place. Israel has returned to a united obedience of the LORD God. Later in the book, we'll see this peace being compromised by disunity and idolatry; but not here.

He Saved... He Died

The Othniel "ideal" cycle, bringing true and full revival to the people of God, is structured so that the emphasis falls on two key phrases. In **verse 7**, the Israelites serve idols. In **verse 8**, God "sold them into the hands" of an enemy, who oppressed them. Then in **verse 9**, he "raised up" a deliverer. This is mirrored by **verse 10**—"he became Israel's judge." Then God "gave" the enemy king "into the hands of Othniel," who oppressed or overpowered him. Finally, the land which began in idolatry and then suffered subjection "had peace."

This structure makes two statements stand out. First, "he saved them" (**v 9**). Restoration and revival only come to God's people when God works through his chosen deliverer. The "peace" of enjoying serving God instead of slaving miserably for false gods comes only through his saving actions. We cannot force or fabricate revival—we can only cry out for God to save.

Second, this episode does not end with peace. It concludes with death. Things went well "until Othniel son of Kenaz died" (**v 11**). Salvation and peace rest on the leadership of God's judge. Othniel is a good judge (the narrative points out no flaws in his character or leadership); the peace is real. But it cannot last, since Othniel does not last. It is only temporary. Cycles of revival throughout church history have been temporary, too. For permanent restoration, and unending peace serving the LORD, God's people need a leader who does not die. **Verse 11** points us to the problem with every human leader of God's church, however Spirit-empowered, and points us to look to One who says to his people: "I am the Living One; I was dead, and behold I am alive for ever and ever!" (Revelation 1:18). The forty years of peace Othniel brought before his death cause us to thank Jesus Christ for the eternal peace he brings us beyond his death.

Questions for reflection

1. How are you making sure you remember in your heart what you know in your head about God?

2. Do you consciously enjoy the "peace" of having been saved from God and freed from slaving for idols? How will you remember to enjoy it this week?

3. "I am the Living One; I was dead, and behold I am alive for ever and ever!" (Revelation 1:18). How does this truth about your Leader make you feel about being a Christian today?

PART TWO

A Left-Handed Rescuer

With Othniel's death (Judges **3:11**), the cycle begins again—"the Isra-elites did evil in the eyes of the Lord" (**v 12**). This time, God gives them over to Eglon, king of Moab. God's people face not simply one king, but an alliance of enemies (**v 13**). And the subjection is worse—"they took possession of the City of Palms" (**v 13**), the city otherwise known as Jericho. This was the place where, supremely, God had given his obedient people victory over their enemies (Joshua 6); now this is the place where God "gave" Eglon victory over them. Further, the subjec-tion is a decade longer (Judges **3:14**).

As in the last cycle, the people respond to God sending trouble by crying out to him (**v 15**). "And he gave them a deliverer—Ehud, a left-handed man." To the first readers of Judges, the greatest surprise in this narrative would have been that Ehud, the man God used, was "left-handed" (**v 15**). If you look up the references in the Bible to "right hand," you will find that they are all quite positive. God swears by his right hand, he has pleasures by his right hand, and his chosen One sits at his right hand (Isaiah 62:8-9; Psalm 16:11; 110:1). Why? Since most people were right-handed, the right hand was a symbol of power and ability. You fought with your sword in your right hand. But Judges **3:15** literally says that Ehud was "unable to use his right hand." It is very possible that Ehud's right hand was paralyzed or disa-bled in some way.

Othniel was a typical "leader-type:" a warrior from a family of faithful men, in the tribe of Judah (who were chosen by God to be "the first to go up" into their inheritance, 1:1-2). Ehud is a surprising choice; in a society which was even more cruel than our own to people who were

> Ehud is a surprising choice—yet he is God's choice.

physically handicapped, he would have been considered ineffective. No one would have looked up to him or naturally chosen to follow him. Yet he is God's choice.

The Right (Left) Man

In fact, though, Ehud is uniquely suited for the task of deliverance God has chosen him for. He is sent "with tribute to Eglon king of Moab" (**3:15**); and we are told what Eglon cannot know—that "Ehud had made a double-edged sword … which he strapped to his right thigh under his clothing" (**v 16**). This introduces tension into the story. Right-handers carried their swords on the left. Will Ehud's sword, hidden on his right side, go undetected? Can he get close enough to Eglon to use it?

In **verse 17**, he cannot. He "presented the tribute to Eglon." But here is added the detail (which later will prove crucial, and quite funny), that Eglon "was a very fat man." Ehud and his delegation leave, but then Ehud sends them on and turns back himself with "a secret message for you, O king!" (**v 19**). We know what the "message" is!

Now we see how Ehud is fitted for his role. "The king said, 'Quiet!' And all his attendants left him." Wilcock points out that Eglon does not expect a handicapped man to be in any way dangerous:

> "If Ehud cannot wield a weapon in his right hand, all assume that he cannot wield one at all. This is why … he is admitted to the presence of the king [when] he asks for a private audience with Eglon. Because of his deformity, he presents no security risk to the Moabite."   (*The Message of Judges*, page 41)

So, sword still hidden on his "wrong side," Ehud approaches the king "while he was sitting alone" to deliver the message (**v 20**). The narrator makes very clear in **verse 21** that it is Ehud's left-handedness that allows him to strike down the tyrant who has demanded payment—tribute—from God's people: "Ehud reached with his *left hand*, drew the sword from his *right thigh* and plunged it into the king's belly" (**v 21**). It is the king's obesity (perhaps he has grown fat on the tribute he has exacted?) which seals his fate (**v 22**). The NIV is over-polite here: the end of the verse should read "the dung came out" (ESV). This explains why, as Ehud mounts his escape (**v 23**), the guards stay outside, assuming (based on what they can smell) that Eglon "must be relieving himself" (**v 24**). By the time they open the doors and see their lord dead (**v 25**), Ehud has "got away … and escaped" (**v 26**).

Many people are unhappy that the chosen agent of God is an assassin, who kills a man having duped him into meeting him alone. Yet Ehud himself says that God was working through him (**v 28**). Israel would never have followed him into battle (**v 28-29**) if he had not secured the outcome himself, alone, by killing Eglon. And it reminds us that God does not always work by what we call "normal" or "obvious" methods. He freed his people, giving them triumph over their enemies and peace for eighty years (**v 30**), through an unexpected leader and an unpredicted means.

> God does not always work by what we call normal methods.

Ehud: God's Type of Leader

Perhaps Ehud teaches us more about how God saves his people than Othniel and Shamgar (**v 31**), the more predictable judges.

After Othniel, we see that each "cyclical" judge (that is, those, unlike Shamgar, whose story is not simply summarized in one or two verses—see also 10:1-5; 12:8-15) is "unexpected" as far as the world is concerned. And we will also see that each judge increasingly has to do the saving him or herself. As Israel's judge, Othniel "went to war" (**3:10**), implicitly with all the fighters among Israel at his back. Ehud struck down the enemy king on his own, before leading "the Israelites" into battle (**v 27-29**). The next judges, Deborah and Barak, together lead only two tribes (4:9-10)—and the last judge, Samson, has to deliver Israel single-handedly (16:29-30).

This all points the way to the most unexpected and "left-handed" person of all. When *the* Judge came, "he had ... nothing in his appearance that we should desire him. He was despised and rejected by men" (Isaiah 53:2-3). He achieved his victory all alone, on behalf of his people but not helped in any way by them. And he crushed his people's enemies through his own weakness, like Ehud.

All of the judges from Ehud onward point us to Christ. Unlike them, he did not use deception (Ehud), need assistance (Deborah/Barak), or display selfish ambition (Gideon), rashness (Jephthah) or sexual weakness (Samson). In fact, he was in every way as flawless as Othniel appears on the pages of Judges. And yet, like all the major judges after Othniel, Jesus was an outsider, someone the world could not believe was either God's chosen Ruler or his Rescuer (see, for example, Luke 23:35-39 and 1 Corinthians 1:18, 22-23). Jesus is still more of an unlikely and inside-out Deliverer. He delivered his people not through great triumph, but through crushing defeat.

> Jesus delivered his people not through great triumph, but through crushing defeat.

In these historical narratives, then, God is showing the world that his salvation will not come in a "hollywood" way at all. It will come from an outsider born in a manger; through weakness, not what the world calls strength; through defeat, not what the world calls victory; through folly, not what the world calls wisdom. We are not to make the mistake Eglon did as he looked at God's chosen deliverer, and "esteem him not" (Isaiah 53:3); we look at Christ and see "the power of God and the wisdom of God" (1 Corinthians 1:24).

Think Of What You Were

Ehud points us to Jesus: he also points us to ourselves. God uses a "left-handed" deliverer... to save "left-handed" people! "Think of what you were when you were called. Not many of you were wise by human standards; not many were influential; not many were of noble birth. But God chose the foolish things…" (1 Corinthians 1:26-27).

God is a God of grace, not works. He takes and uses people who are at the margins of society—in order to show that salvation is from him, not from our own human ability. Paul says that God tends to choose and use people who are weaker socially, physically, and even morally. Why? "So that no human being might boast in the presence of God" (v 29, ESV).

Knowing this shatters the very heart of the "idolatry **mindset**" which we often bring to our worship of the true God. If we worship an idol, we are trying to stay fully in control of our lives, negotiating with the idol-god, giving it what it wants so that it gives us what we want. It is not loving submission, but cynical **manipulation**. In this idol-mindset, it is critical that worship be a reliable, consistent technique. We have to know that if we do *X* for the idol, then *Y* will result. How easy it is to treat God like that! *If I do X, he will save me.* Or, more subtly: *If I do X, he will bless me.*

But when we truly turn to God, we see that he demands heart surrender, not partial concessions and negotiations. We do not do deals with God, because we have nothing to offer him. We "think of what we were." We learn that he has already saved us and blessed us in the most unexpected way—through a "left-hander," and that we are the most unexpected recipients of his grace, "left-handed" as we are. We realize that we can only totally depend on

> We do not do deals with God, because we have nothing to offer him.

God, and we love to do that. As the old hymn by Augustus Toplady, *Rock of Ages,* puts it:

> *Nothing in my hand I bring,*
> *Simply to thy cross I cling.*

Questions for reflection

1. When in your own experience have you seen God using unexpected people and/or unpredictable means to do great things?

2. "Think of what you were..." How are you "left-handed"? How does this humble you?

3. Do you ever try to do deals with God? How do you need simply to surrender to him, and enjoy the rescue he freely gives to you?

4. DEBORAH AND BARAK: RULER AND RESCUER

Chapters 4 and 5 of Judges are very interesting, not only because of the events they describe, but because each chapter deals with the same events; one from the perspective of the historian, and the other from the perspective of the poet. We will spend most of our time in chapter 4, and then notice how the flavors and emphases in the next chapter's song provide us with a richer, deeper perspective.

A Godly Ruler

With the death of Ehud, "the Israelites once again did evil in the eyes of the LORD" (**4:1**). So the cycle begins once more, with Israel finding themselves under the heel of Jabin, a king of Canaan (**v 2**)—a ruler who, if Israel had trusted and obeyed God fully back in chapter 1, would not even have been there. Jabin's main agent of oppression is Sisera, his commander, who has "nine hundred iron chariots" (the smartbombs and drones of the age) at his disposal (**v 3**). The oppression is worse than either Cushan-Rishathaim's or Eglon's; it is "cruel," and it lasts twenty years (**v 3**). And so Israel "cried to the LORD for help."

Enter "Deborah, a prophetess" (**v 4**). As a prophetess, she preaches and teaches the word of God (we see her doing this in **verse 6**: "The LORD, the God of Israel, commands you..."). And she is "leading Israel" (**v 4**)—"she held court." This is not a queen's court; rather, it is an actual courtroom, where Israelites would come to have their "disputes decided" (**v 5**). Clearly, she was recognized as a wise counselor and judge, and people came to her to settle all sorts of social, legal and relational cases.

In this way, Deborah is very different from all the other judges, before and after her. She led from wisdom and character, rather than sheer might. Where Othniel "went to war" (3:10) and Ehud made his assassination plan (3:16), Deborah counseled and guided the people. So she comes closest to being a godly *leader* of the people, instead of simply a general. She was a judge who led beyond the battlefield. In all this, we are reminded that God's chosen leader does not simply rescue, but also rules. Deborah was in this sense the greatest pointer to the monarchy and even the Christ, who can bear the government on his shoulders, and is called "Wonderful Counselor … Prince of Peace … establishing and upholding [his kingdom] with justice and righteousness" (Isaiah 9:6-7).

> God's chosen leader does not simply rescue, but also rules.

A Godly Rescuer

In fact, Deborah is (alone among the judges) *not* a warrior. She is not the one who, in God's strength, rescues Israel by defeating her oppressors. Instead, "she sent for Barak" (Judges **4:6**), and passed on God's commission to him. It is Barak who is to take 10,000 men to Mount Tabor (**v 6**), and it is he to whom God will give victory over Sisera (**v 7**).

The ruler will not be the rescuer; and the rescuer is not the ruler. And, as we'll see in verses 17-21, neither Deborah nor Barak will be the one who has the honor of removing the main enemy, Sisera. In every other case, from Othniel on through to Samson, there is only one single human "hero." Here, there are three. And, as we will see in the song of chapter 5, this means that we can see where the ultimate honor should go: not to one, or two, or three people used by God (though it is a blessing to be given such a privilege, 5:24), but to the LORD, who works through those whom he chooses to rescue and rule his people.

Barak's response to God's call through Deborah, and Deborah's reply to him, have been read in two ways; one more pessimistic about Barak, the other more optimistic.

1. The more pessimistic view sees Barak asking Deborah to go with him, and refusing to go if she doesn't (**4:8**), as a timid lack of faith. This makes sense of the way the NIV renders **verse 9**: Deborah agrees to go with him, "but because of the way you are going about this [ie: refusing simply to trust and obey God], the honor will not be yours, for the LORD will hand Sisera over to a woman." Barak then summons the troops and prepares to fight, but only because Deborah is with him (**v 9, 10**). It's not until **verse 14**— *after* Sisera has gathered his awesome war machine (**v 12-13**) and Deborah has again told Barak to "Go! This is the day the LORD has given Sisera into your hands. Has not the LORD gone ahead of you?"—that Barak charges down Mount Tabor with his men. It's only at that point that he shows the faith he is commended for in Hebrews 11:32; and so the withholding of honor in Judges **4:9** is a rebuke to Barak for his lack of obedient, radical faith in **verse 8**.

2. The more optimistic view rests on the fact that the Hebrew in **verse 9** can also be translated as: "On the expedition you are undertaking, the honor will not be yours…" (as the NIV footnote has it). So Deborah is not rebuking Barak, but simply telling him that though he will have to charge down the hillside into the teeth of nine hundred iron chariots, he will not get the honor for it! It's a prophetic statement of fact, not a verdict on his faith.

On this reading, which I favor, Barak is a hero and example of faith not only in **verse 14**, but throughout. His desire to take Deborah with him is not disobedience, but done out of a recognition that Deborah is a godly woman who speaks God's words. Why wouldn't he want her with him?! So first, Barak shows us that faith is listening to God at every stage of life, and in every circumstance.

Second, faith is showing courage in the face of humanly over-whelming odds. An iron chariot could cut through foot-soldiers like a hot knife through butter. Nine hundred chariots would beat 10,000 men every time. But Barak still fights.

Third, faith is humble and not honor-seeking. He obeys God and leads his men down the mountain, knowing that the victory will be given to another, and that the rule will not be his afterwards. In his faith, Barak fore-shadows the great Deliverer, who though in very nature God (the rightful Ruler, unlike Barak), still "did not consider equality with God something to be grasped, but made himself nothing … he humbled himself and became obedient to death—even death on a cross!" (Philippians 2:6-8).

On Mount Tabor, as God's obedient servant goes into battle against an enemy who seems to hold all the aces (nine hundred of them), "the LORD routed Sisera and all his chariots … by the sword" (Judges **4:15**). Barak's forces were no match for Sisera's; but Sisera's were no match for God! Sisera, so secure in his chariots, abandons his own (**v 15**); and all his troops "fell by the sword" (**v 16**). The victory is almost complete; all that remains is for Barak to catch up with the fleeing Sisera. But by the time he does, Sisera will be dead.

Deborah and Women's Ministry

Before we see Sisera's gruesome end, we need to pause for a while and bring up the topic of women's leadership, because the career of Deborah very obviously leads us to reflect on this subject.

A few words of clarification and caution are helpful here. First, this is not a large enough space to deal exhaustively with this area. Second, we must read passages within the context of the book, the Testament, and the Bible of which they are a part. Third, we should be cautious of reading narrative—the record of what happened—over-prescriptively, as a record of what *should* happen. Fourth, we should use clear teaching in Scripture to help inform our view of more cloudy passages.

In considering Deborah, the third "caution" is a good place to start. Judges 4 and 5 are written simply to tell us what happened, not what should have happened (and far less what ought to happen today). So what we could call a "traditionalist" view of women's roles will call this an **anomaly**, caused by the timid abdication of responsibility of the men (such as Barak). Men should be in leadership; Deborah has to step in because they won't. But the chapter does not say this. In fact, Deborah is clearly called by God to be a dispute-settler and prophet-ess. It is an **inference**, and it is always unwise to draw firm doctrine from vague inference.

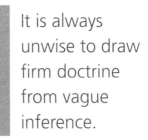

It is always unwise to draw firm doctrine from vague inference.

But the "liberal" view—which insists that "anything a man can do, a woman can do," dismissing gender differences as socially constructed fictions—is also challenged. Deborah, alone among the judges, does not fight—she is not a warrior, cannot lead the army, and has to recruit someone whose abilities will complement hers (which she does admirably).

Further, the issue is complicated by the fact that Israel, at this point in history, was both a civil state and the people of God. There are aspects of Israel's Old Testament life which refer to Israel being a state (eg: the punishments for committing crimes), and which are still functions of the state today, but not of the church (God's people); other aspects are now functions of the church, but not of the state (eg: celebrating the Passover/Lord's Supper). So even if we take it (as I do) from Deborah's career that there is no reason why women should not lead in civil roles (business, politics, etc), that does not mean that we *must* carry that over into the life of God's gathered people today—the church.

This is where the second caution is helpful. In Old Testament Israel, there were three great "offices:" prophet, priest and leader (king/judge). Some women (such as Deborah) were prophets; some were judges/queens (Deborah again!). None were priests (Numbers 3:10 and Leviticus 21 show that all priests were men, descended from Aaron). The Old Testament tells us that women are equal in value, dignity and ability, created as they are in God's image and given dominion under him over his creation (Genesis 1:26-28). It also shows us that women were free to use their gifts in any role but that of priest. God shows his Old Testament people that men and women are equal, but not equivalent.

The New Testament and Women's Ministry

This is a pattern we find in the New Testament, too. Women serve God as prophets and as **deacons** (1 Timothy 3:11—even if these are deacons' wives rather than "deaconesses," it is important that there are qualifications for this role, whereas there are no qualifications for being an elder's/overseer's/bishop's wife in verses 1-7). God reserves one role for men (1 Timothy 3:1): the role of elder/overseer/bishop (depending on the church polity—for ease, and as a Presbyterian, I will simply call this role "elder" from now on).

This is why Paul—having assumed that women will speak in public in church meetings, both prophesying and praying (1 Corinthians 11:5)—then tells women to "keep silent" in the church (1 Corinthians 14:34). This cannot mean literal verbal wordlessness throughout the meeting; the context isn't public ministry in general, but the evaluation of the doctrine of a speaker. When someone speaks, there must be "others" who "weigh carefully what is said" (v 29), to declare it true or false—in other words, to have disciplinary authority. This is the role of the elders; and so at this point, "women should remain silent."

This is also what Paul is teaching in 1 Timothy 2:11-12, when he says women should not "teach or have authority." The question here is whether Paul is forbidding two things to women—teaching *and* authority—or one thing, expressed in two phrases (a *hendiadys*—like when we say "the baby is nice and cosy," we mean the same thing, twice—not that the baby has an even temperament, *and* is warm). I take the latter view (because the Greek linking word, *oude*, often joins expressions which are mutually defining). This squares with the other New Testament evidence—that women did teach, but did not teach with disciplinary power.

To summarize, the New Testament pattern is the same as the Old. Women are free to use their gifts in every role except the one God has reserved for men: priests in the Old Testament, and then those who teach-with-authority in the New (this is not to say that these roles are directly equivalent). This guards us against wrong extremes in both directions (just as Deborah's career does). God forbids *one* kind of role in the church to women, as he did in Israel. So we must not jump to forbidding *all* teaching and tasks to women; and we shouldn't assert all sorts of specific tasks are off-limits (eg: working outside the home, not teaching males over 12, not speaking from the front in services, etc). Nowhere does the Bible give such details; it is better to say that women can do everything that a man who isn't an elder can do. Equally, God *does* forbid one role to women in the church. This is *not* to say women are any less valuable, since our value as humans lies in being made in the image of God, not in what we do (otherwise a president would be intrinsically more valuable than someone who is unemployed).

Another (final!) word of caution. How the biblical principle of "equal but not equivalent" is worked out in churches will vary depending on church polity, temperament, and culture. We must not be too quick to judge those whose practice is different; nor even those whose principles are different.

> We must not be too quick to judge those whose practice is different.

Those against women's **ordination** are often condemning and cold to those who differ with them—in other words, not treating them as brothers and sisters in Christ. On the other hand, those who do believe in women's ordination may be similarly unaccepting. They may think of opponents as being sexist in a manner which is as scandalous as racism.

But God has given us unity around the doctrines he has in his wisdom chosen to make crystal clear—the deity of Christ, his Triune nature, the need for grace for forgiveness, the **inerrancy** of Scripture, and so on. We should not give up that unity because we can't agree on issues such as baptism, church government, speaking in tongues, and so on. The question of women's roles is one of these ongoing issues. The church will likely never come to consensus about it. We must treat it as important, but not a cause for abrasive condemnations. We want people with different views on this to be able to live together. That would make our churches very, very unusual. If we were able to say: *I disagree with you, but I agree with you on what is truly important, you are my brother and sister, and we will serve and worship together*, then we would model to the world a much needed picture of unity, and of Christ-like love.

Questions for reflection

1. What do you do differently in your life because you have faith, even though you don't get honor for doing it?

2. Are there times you can look back on when you have taken a risk in obeying the Lord, and found him providing what you need as you do so? Are there ways in which you are/should be doing that now?

3. What are your reflections on the role of women in the church? Do you think you are more likely to be influenced by unbiblical traditionalism, or unbiblical liberalism?

PART TWO

Death by Tent Peg

There is a deliciously inexplicable break in the narrative of Barak's victory over Sisera in Judges **4:11**. 10,000 men stand ready for battle (**v 10**)… Sisera is about to summon his charioteers (**v 12-13**)… and the narrator tells us that "Heber the Kenite had left the other Kenites, the descendants of Hobab, Moses' brother-in-law, and pitched his tent" near the battleground (**v 11**). We're not told why he did this, and he plays no part in the battle. His wife, however, suddenly becomes integral to the plot.

Sisera, fleeing on foot, reaches "the tent of Jael," which means safety, because Jabin and Heber are allies (**v 17**). Yet, with echoes of Ehud's assassination of Eglon, Jael, having welcomed him, given him a drink, and let him go to sleep (**v 18-21**), "picked up a tent peg and a hammer … [and] drove the peg through his temple into the ground" (**v 21**). We hardly need the next three words: "and he died"!

The method of Jael's attack on Sisera deepens the irony of the passage even further. Setting up and taking down tents was considered the work of women. Therefore, the tent peg and hammer were essentially a woman's household appliance! In that age, death at the hand of a woman was particularly humiliating, of course. All this was probably designed by Jael to make Sisera's death the most devastating defeat possible.

It also means that Deborah's prophecy back in verse 9 is shown to be true. The honor will not be Barak's; it will not be hers, either (she is not the woman to whom God hands Sisera over). When Barak passes Jael's tent, she promises to "show you the man you're looking for" (**v 22**). We can imagine Barak, sword in hand, entering the tent protectively in front of Jael, to discover him on the ground, dead, with a tent peg through his head.

Humanly speaking, the honor has been shared. But really, the honor goes to no human at all. It was the LORD who spoke to, and through,

Deborah; the LORD who went ahead of Barak and then gave him victory (**v 14-15**); and the LORD who handed Sisera over to Jael (**v 9**). It is a fair conclusion to say that "on that day, God [not Deborah, Barak or Jael] subdued Jabin, the Canaanite king, before the Israelites" (**v 23**). God is the Rescuer, acting according to his will, not his people's merits; so he deserves the glory. His working through people is a privilege for them, not a praise-earner; and salvation is all of God's doing, all "according to the will of our God and Father" so it is him "to whom [should] be glory for ever and ever" (Galatians 1:4-5).

Nevertheless, we cannot overlook the fact that Jael's method is a clear violation of two of the Ten Commandments (she lies and she kills). Some would say that since she was not a believer, she was not responsible to obey God's law. But Jael also broke all the very strong policies and rules of Middle Eastern hospitality. It was treachery by the standards of any culture. We have to remember that God often uses people to do what he wants to happen without violating their personal responsibility or condoning their methods.

God Wins

With Jabin destroyed (**4:24**), we should expect to read of peace for Israel in the land. And we do (**5:31**); but not until we have read of the same events, but from a different angle. The foundational difference in chapter 5 is that this is a song, and the approach is more **theological**. It looks beneath the surface of the history and reveals that God's hand, hinted at in chapter 4, was behind it all.

In chapter 4, the LORD is named only in four verses, three of those as Deborah speaks (4:6, 9, 14—the other is in v 15); in chapter 5, he is everywhere. He receives the praise and singing as Deborah and Barak (**5:1**) sing of the "princes" (ie: chiefs) of Israel leading their men (**v 2-3**). Why? Because as they marched, crucially he was on the march, showing his power through pouring rain (**v 4**). As his people advanced down the mountain, the One before whom mountains quake was going to war (**v 5**).

This is because he is the true God, which is the message of the next verse of the song. "The roads were abandoned" in Israel (**v 6**) and "village life in Israel ceased" (**v 7**) because "they chose new gods [and so] war came to the city gates" (**v 8**). Under idol-worship, Israel fell under oppression but also into social decay. The cessation of "village life" meant it was every family, even every man, for themselves. The only hope lay in Deborah, who "mothered" Israel, beginning to restore the social fabric (**v 7**) and then prompting the "willing volunteers among the people" to go to war to throw off the oppression (**v 9**). Their actions would be, as we've seen, really God's actions (**v 10-11**)—**verses 11b-12** suggest that it was not only Deborah calling for a leader to rise up against Sisera.

Verses 13-18 reveal that not all Israel rallied to Barak's banner. Some from the tribes of Ephraim and Benjamin did, as did Issachar (**v 14-15**). But Reuben carried on herding sheep (**v 15-16**); and Gilead, Dan and Asher stayed home, too (**v 17**). The greatest honor goes to Zebulun and Naphtali; to those who "risked their very lives … on the heights of the field" (**v 18**).

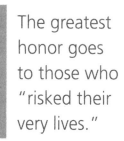

The greatest honor goes to those who "risked their very lives."

Now, in **verses 19-22**, Deborah and Barak return to the theme with which they began—that this was the LORD's victory. "The kings of Canaan fought"— but they won no plunder, because they won no victory (**v 19**). The God who rules nature—even the stars—was fighting against them (**v 20**). And **verse 21** reveals how it was that Sisera's unbeatable chariots were rendered useless. The God who made the "clouds pour down water" (**v 4**) caused the river to flood, sweeping them away as Barak advanced (**v 21**). Here, though, Barak is not even mentioned! Truly this was God's victory. Sisera would never have arranged his chariots next to a river if he had been expecting rain. This must have been the dry season, not the wet; but God, through Deborah, told Israel just where to fight (4:6), luring Sisera's army to the place where he would destroy them (v 7, **5:21-22**).

What is the lesson for God's people? That God wins—and so blessing is to be found in fighting for and with him, putting ourselves in his service whatever the odds or likely cost. Conversely, there is a curse for those who do the opposite—who stay at home (**v 23**). It is not that the LORD requires help (the song has shown that beyond doubt!) but that the LORD allows his people to "help." And so "most blessed of women be Jael" (**v 24**), who, despite being a Kenite and not an Israelite, took her place in the story and killed God's enemy (**v 24-27**).

> Blessing is to be found in fighting for God, whatever the odds or cost.

Deborah pictures Sisera's mother and her ladies-in-waiting looking for him to return victorious. As they discuss how the campaign "should" go, we learn that Sisera likes to steal and rape and enslave women (**v 28-30**), which they think accounts for his delayed return. The NIV translation "girl" in **verse 30** is unhelpful; the Hebrew is closer to "wench" or "girl-slave." Sisera captured girls to make them sex slaves.

This whole Judges cycle is framed around the actions of women: Deborah leads Israel under Sisera's oppression, seen most horribly in how he treats Israel's women; and Jael, another woman, is the means by which his reign of rape and terror is ended. After making the lives of many women hellish nightmares, it is two women who bring him down. There is great irony that the man who used women as objects is killed by a womanly object. "So may all your enemies perish, O LORD," concludes the woman who has led, and will continue to lead, Israel (**v 31**). "Then the land had peace forty years."

Living with Two Perspectives

Setting Judges 4 and 5 alongside one another, the narrator encourages us to have a chapter 5 perspective on our own lives, as well as a chapter 4 one. Chapter 5 sees God's hand behind all things; celebrates success and honors him supremely; and has a continual note of praise.

We can, and should, live our lives and order our memories not only historically but theologically—not simply recollecting what happened, or what we did, but searching out what God was doing. This keeps us from over-honoring ourselves in success, or despairing in our struggles. Part of the key to enjoying peace is to be continually praising the Lord for what he has done, and is doing, for us, because the story we tell of our lives is not so much about us, as about him.

What about loving our enemies?!

It's noticeable how fierce and bloodthirsty this song is, which raises the broader issue of how often Old Testament texts (especially some of the psalms) seem to speak hatefully of enemies. How can that square with Jesus' command to love, bless and pray for our enemies (Luke 6:27-28)?

Three things are worth saying on this issue. First, God's triumph over evil, and the fact that one day all people will stand before him and be held to account for their actions, are aspects of the gospel message which we should welcome and rejoice over (though we tremble as we do so, knowing that we will stand there as well, with Jesus alone as our **advocate**). The New Testament is quite clear that Jesus should be praised for his victory over sin and Satan, and for his final judgment (eg: Revelation 11:15-18).

Second, though, coming judgment frees us from needing to see justice done in this life. There will be **vindication** of those who have acted rightly, and punishment of wrongdoing, beyond this life. We do not need to seek them now: "Do not take revenge, my friends, but leave room for God's wrath, for it is written: 'It is mine to avenge; I will repay,' says the Lord" (Romans 12:19, referencing Deuteronomy 32:35). We are free to get on with going out of our way to bless those who curse us (v 14, 20).

How can we know that God is a God who will "repay"? Because, thirdly, we have seen sin judged already, on the cross. The cross is not only the place where we are **justified**; it is the proof that God *does* judge and punish sin (Romans 3:25-26). And the resurrection tells us that there will be a judgment for all those whose sin has not been punished in the Lord Jesus' death; it is the proof that God *will* judge and punish sin (Acts 17:31).

The death and resurrection of Christ fundamentally change our attitude toward our enemies. We want to see justice done, and we know that it will be—but not by us (of course, the Old Testament believers could only have a much dimmer view of this). We can yearn for that, while still praying for and blessing our enemies. *Because of* the cross, we can have the attitude Jesus had *on* the cross, as he looked at those who were killing him and said: "Father, forgive them" (Luke 23:34).

Questions for reflection

1. How is it encouraging, and humbling, to know that God works through flawed people?

2. What happens if we only have a Judges 4 perspective on our life? What difference would it make to you if you always maintained both a Judges 4 and Judges 5 perspective?

3. Are there any ways you need to leave justice to God, and get on with loving, blessing and praying for your enemies? How will you use the cross to free you to do this?

5. GIDEON: THE WEAK MIGHTY WARRIOR

"Again the Israelites did evil in the eyes of the Lᴏʀᴅ" (**v 1**). We are now becoming wearily familiar with the beginning of another "Judges cycle," as God's people fail to heart-remember who he is and what he has done, and turn to worship idols (which is what it means to "do evil"). This time, the cycle will cover three chapters, both of the book of Judges and in this book. Since the essential stages of the cycle are now familiar to us, the narrative encourages us to look at the particular details of this cycle, and any differences in it.

Sermon Before Salvation

This time, God "gave them into the hands of the Midianites" (**v 1**). It is the worst oppression yet—Israelites are forced to leave their homes and "[prepare] shelters for themselves" in the inaccessible mountain ranges (**v 2**). The Midianites were not interested in political control but rather economic exploitation, plundering the land of its crops (**v 3**). They "did not spare a living thing for Israel" (**v 4**)—the people were starving and the land was ravaged (**v 5**). Eventually, "Midian so impoverished the Israelites that they cried out to the Lᴏʀᴅ" (**v 6**).

So far, though more oppressive, the cycle is following its normal route. Now we expect God to raise up a deliverer, a judge (as in 3:9, 15; 4:4, 6-7). But instead, "when the Israelites cried to the Lᴏʀᴅ because of Midian, he sent them a prophet" (**6:7-8**). God's first response to the people's cry is *not* to send a savior or salvation, but to give them a sermon! Before they can appreciate the rescue that will come, the people need to understand why they need rescuing. The prophet comes and helps them to understand why they are in the trouble they are in. He wants them to understand where their idolatry—their sin—has led them.

The nature of the sermon shows that God is trying to convict the people so that they will be truly repentant—which suggests that the "crying out" of **verses 6-7** is not a sign of real repentance. Their history, after the deaths of Othniel, Ehud and Deborah, is strong evidence that their sorrow was skin-deep, not heartfelt. So God reminds them of two things: what he has done, and what they have done. What has he done? *I rescued you out of Egypt, freeing you from slavery. I took you out of all oppression, and I gave you this land by driving out your enemies. I repeatedly reminded you that I am the Lord, and that I am your God, who demands and deserves your exclusive obedience. And so I told you not to worship other "gods"* (**v 8-10**). What has Israel done? "You have not listened to me" (**v 10**).

God sends the prophet to convict of sin *before* he sends the judge to rescue from oppression because the people are regretful, but not repentant. The Bible makes a clear distinction between the two: "Godly sorrow brings repentance that leads to salvation and leaves no regret, but worldly sorrow brings death" (2 Corinthians 7:10). Both are characterized by very deep sorrow and distress. But they are completely different. First, "worldly" sorrow or regret does not produce any real change, while repentance does. Why? Regret is sorrow over the consequences of a sin, but not over the sin itself. If there had been no consequences, there would have been no sorrow. There is no sorrow over the sin for what it is in itself, for how it grieves God and violates our relationship with him. The focus is all horizontal—"worldly"—and not at all

> The focus of regret is all horizontal— "worldly"— and not at all vertical.

vertical—concerned about how it affects relationship with God. Therefore, as soon as the consequences go away, the behavior comes back. The heart has not become disgusted with the sin itself, so the sin remains rooted.

Second, "worldly" sorrow stays regretful, while repentance removes all regret about the past. Why? Real repentance comes to focus on the only real, permanent result of sin—the "loss" of the Lord. Repentance always makes us more able to accept and "move past" the things that happened. When we realize that God has forgiven us and we haven't "lost" him, we feel that earthly results are rather small in comparison. We say: *I deserved far worse than what happened. The real punishment fell on Jesus, and will never come to me.*

After real repentance and restoration to God, we do not hate ourselves, and we do not hate our lives. When someone is inconsolable, it means they have made something besides God their real god and savior (eg: money, friends, career, family). It is an idol, and its loss is therefore impossible to heal without **repudiating** it as an idol.

> When someone is inconsolable, it means they have made something besides God into their savior.

Regret is all about "us:" how I am being hurt, how my life is ruined, how my heart is breaking; but repentance is all about God: how he has been grieved, how his nature as Creator and Redeemer is being trampled on, how his repeated saving actions are being trivialized and used manipulatively.

We know the people of Israel are idolators. God's response to their crying shows that they are regretful for what they have lost, and want it restored; but they are not repenting of their idolatry. God's aim in sending them his prophet is to move them beyond regret to repentance.

What can we learn from this? Many things! Most importantly, to check what we are sorry about: the consequences of the sin in our lives, or the sin itself; the loss of the pleasure an idol offered, or the damage to our relationship with God. Here are two other implications:

- We have to listen to God's word. It is interesting that the people cried out for some dramatic miracle, and God sent them a sermon—an exposition of the word of God. There is no getting around the study of the Bible. That is where we learn who we are; that is the means through which God brings spiritual renewal in our lives.

- We need to discern in ourselves the difference between the normal lapses on the road to increasing Christian maturity and getting "stuck"—a repeated pattern of lapses which is a sign of no real progress. If you are continually falling into the same spiritual pit, and your falls are not decreasing in numbers or intensity, then you may be responding in regret rather than repentance. In other words, you may be simply regretful for the troubles of your sin, but unwilling to identify and reject the idol under the sin which is still attractive to you. The big problem here is that we often cannot get a good perspective on our hearts all by ourselves. Many people who are making progress feel they are not, and many people who are not making progress are in denial about it. This is why we need several strong Christian friends and Christian leaders who can help us tell the difference.

Grace Before Repentance

Does Israel respond by repenting? There is no sign of it! Judges **6:11** does not tell us of the people's heartfelt repentance, the burning of their idols, and so on. Instead, "the angel of the LORD came and sat down ... where ... Gideon was **threshing** wheat in a winepress to keep it from the Midianites" (a small detail which pictures superbly the level of fear under which the Israelites are laboring). God is commissioning his judge—even though the people have not repented. God does not wait for us to repent before he begins to save us—"while we were still sinners, Christ died for us" (Romans 5:8). God does not begin to save us because we repent. We repent *because* he's begun his saving work in us, through the external work of his Son and the internal work of his Spirit.

These verses show us the wonderful truth that God is both more holy and more merciful than we are. He responds to a cry for help by sending a prophet to tell them about their sin, to explain why they are in the mess they are. This seems a much more severe response than we would give someone begging for mercy—and yet, of course, if someone keeps slipping into a river and nearly drowning, it is loving to point out their foolishness for continuing to walk close to the edge of the bank! And God goes forth to recruit and prepare his rescuer even though there is no evidence of real repentance. This is a much more gracious response than we would give someone who continually hurt us and showed no sign of stopping.

> God is both more holy and more merciful than we are.

God will never compromise on his holiness, nor on his grace. Yet often we exclusively emphasize one at the expense of the other (*God would never accept me/them after doing that* or *God is pure love, and accepts everyone no matter what*); or, in our day-to-day experience, we constantly run from one to the other. The way to hold together, and appreciate, both God's perfect standards and his endless compassion is to grasp more deeply the cross of Christ, where the two meet so gloriously.

Questions for reflection

1. Are there things in your past or present about which you're regretful, but not repentant? Will you repent?

2. Is there an area of your life where you are crying out for salvation, but actually God is prompting you to listen to a sermon of some sort first?

3. How does the knowledge that God is acting in grace even before we turn back to him motivate you to repent and listen to him?

PART TWO

The rest of chapter six comprises three parts: a conversation between Gideon and the angel of the LORD; the building and destruction of two altars; a conversation between Gideon and God.

If God is with Us, Why...?

The first conversation concerns two different understandings of Israel's problem and Gideon's ability.

In response to the angel's opening assurance: "The LORD is with you" (Judges **6:12**), Gideon suggests that he isn't! His argument is: *God clearly isn't with us, because he has put us into Midian's hands instead of rescuing us like he did our ancestors.* Of course, we (the readers) know that God put them into the hands of Midian because he had *not* abandoned them, and so was working in their circumstances to show them the poverty of idolatry and to cause them to cry out to him in repentance and for rescue. God's point has already been made, in verses 9-10, through his prophet: *I have not abandoned you, but you have abandoned me.* Now, in response to Gideon's implicit suggestion that they need an Egypt-style rescuer, another Moses, God says: **You** *are the salvation I am sending.* **You** *are my mighty warrior (**v 12**).* **You** *are the Moses for this generation of my people.*

How easy it is for us to make both of Gideon's mistakes! First, we tend to see our troubles as evidence that God has left us, instead of asking how God is working in and through them for our good, as he promises to (Romans 8:28). Second, we are often waiting for God to do something *to* us or *for* us, or wondering why he doesn't use someone to bring help. We essentially say: *Lord, why don't you remove this problem?* instead of saying: *Lord, please make me the person who can handle this problem.*

So God tells Gideon that he is the one who is being sent to "save Israel out of Midian's hand. Am I not sending you?" (Judges **6:14**). This provokes the second "disagreement." Gideon objects that he is "the least in my family" (**v 15**)—he is, economically and socially, the poorest member of the weakest clan of a non-prominent Israelite tribe. "how can [he] save Israel?" (**v 15**).

Yet the angel has already very pointedly called Gideon a "mighty warrior" (**v 12**). Why? Gideon is the kind of man who hides fearfully in a winepress to thresh his wheat! Some think God is mocking Gideon—crouching in that winepress is hardly the action of a fearless warrior! Others suggest that Gideon is being deliberately modest (*Who? Me? No, I couldn't possibly!*), or that he just hasn't realized how much potential he has.

But all of these fail to take seriously either God's power, or his word. If God says Gideon is a mighty warrior, then he is. He is to use his own abilities (**v 14**). But Gideon's potential (realized or not) is not alone sufficient. It needs to be combined with the knowledge that "I [am] sending you … I will be with you" (**v 14, 16**). Gideon is correct to suggest that he cannot save Israel—in his own strength. God is correct to tell him that he will save Israel—using his own strength, combined with knowing that God has called him to this task, and is with him in it. As God's people today, we need the same attitude in the areas of service to which God has called us.

The Angel of the Lord—Who is He?

It is well worth pausing here to ask: Who exactly is the angel of the Lord? We meet the angel several times in Judges (2:1-3, 13:3-21, and here), and throughout the Old Testament (eg: Genesis 18; Exodus 3; 34; Joshua 5:13-15). In appearance, the angel of the Lord does not seem to have been all that overwhelming. It is not until the miracle of Judges **6:21** that Gideon is sure that this is a divine figure. So this is a very human-appearing figure. But there is a remarkable mystery and "tension" in all the biblical descriptions of who the angel is.

On the one hand, we are told "the angel … said" (**v 12, 20**); but we are also told "the Lord said" (**v 14, 16, 18**). Perhaps the angel is a communication channel, a kind of divine speaker-phone?! But then we run into **verse 14**: "The LORD turned to him and said…"

This is remarkable (and confusing!). This figure is the angel of the LORD, and yet also the LORD. What does this mean? This is one of the mysteries of the Old Testament which is impossible to understand without the New. If there is one God, how can he both be in heaven, having *sent* this visible figure, and at the same time *be* the visible figure? If this was simply God come in human form, why doesn't it just say he is the LORD, rather than also one sent by the LORD? (The word "angel" means messenger.)

The only explanation that makes sense is that we have here an indication that our one God is nonetheless multi-personal. We have a deep hint of the **Trinity**. There is good reason to see this figure as God the Son. His concern even then was to bring salvation and peace to his people.

Two Altars

The final evidence that the angel of the LORD is an uncreated, divine person is Gideon's reaction to him. In **verse 16**, it is "the LORD" who "answered." And "Gideon replied" by wanting a sign that "it is really you"—really God himself (**v 17**). He wants to "bring my offering and set it before you" (**v 18-20**); and it is then burned up by the angel, who disappears (**v 21**).

Gideon now knows for sure exactly who he has been talking with: "Ah, Sovereign LORD! I have seen the angel of the LORD face to face!" (**v 22**). In seeing the angel, he has seen God himself—and God has to reassure him that he won't die (**v 23**).

Gideon's response is one of enormous gratitude. He knows that he should have perished, having looked upon the face of the holy God (see Exodus 33:20). But he also knows that somehow, God has provided grace so that he can be at peace with him. "So Gideon built an altar to the LORD there and called it The LORD is Peace" (Judges **6:24**).

He no longer thinks God has abandoned his people to oppression, but that he is with his people to give them peace as they worship him.

Gideon has built an altar to the true, saving God; now he must tear one down which is used to serve a false god, replacing it with one dedicated to the LORD (**v 25-26**). And this altar belongs to *his own father.*

It is no surprise that Joash has an altar and a pole for the worshiping of Canaanite **deities**. While he had clearly taught his children about the exodus from Egypt and the LORD who had rescued their forefathers (**v 13**), he had also chosen to serve Baal and Asherah (**v 25**). The Israelites had not abandoned worship of God *for* idols. They had *combined* the worship of God *with* idols. They worshiped God formally, but in fact their lives revolved around agricultural idols (if they were farmers), or commerce idols (if they were in business), or sex-and-beauty idols, and so on. Michael Wilcock is worth quoting at some length here:

> "The gods have not changed, for human nature has not changed, and these are the gods that humanity regularly re-creates for itself. What does it want? If it is modest—security and comfort and reasonable enjoyment; if ambitious—power and wealth and unbridled self-indulgence. In every age there are forces at work which promise to meet our desires—whether political programs, economic theories, career options, philosophies, lifestyle options, entertainment programs—all having one feature in common. They promise that they can make our lives better than we can make them ourselves, yet at the same time they appear amenable to our manipulating them so we can get what we want without losing our independence …

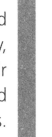

They worshiped God formally, but their lives revolved around idols.

here is the enemy among us. We say we worship the Lord…
but the world has crept in and controls our heart."

(The Message of Judges, pages 80-81)

Before they can throw off the enemies around them (the Midianites), they have to throw off the enemies among them (the false idols of Canaan). This is always the main way that we get renewal in our lives. God will not help us out of your obvious, visible problems (money problems, relationship problems, etc) until we see the idols that we are worshiping right beside the LORD. They have to be removed first.

Gideon is essentially being told here to make God the Lord of every area of life. We are not to add anything to Jesus Christ as a requirement for being happy. We are not to use God to get what we really want, but we are to see and make God the One we really want.

Gideon begins to ally his strength with the LORD's presence, "and did as the LORD told him," albeit at night (**v 27**). The reaction is swift, and it looks as though Gideon's end will be too (**v 28-30**). But Joash stands up for his son—Baal, if he is a divine being, will be able to look after himself (**v 31**). In giving him a nickname of "Let Baal contend with him" (**v 32**), the villagers inadvertently point to the central struggle which continually repeats itself in Israel; the choice between following God's chosen deliverer and leader, and the false gods of the surrounding nations. The LORD will contend with Baal for the hearts of the people, as the LORD's Spirit-filled judge contends with the idol-worshiping "eastern peoples" (**v 33-35**).

The Famous Fleeces

Still Gideon is unsure of God's calling and promise (**v 36**). So he sets out a fleece and asks God to confirm his plans by making it dewy on dry ground (**v 37**)—and then asks God to re-confirm by reversing the request (**v 39**), both of which God does (**v 38, 40**). Many people have criticized Gideon for this action. If, however, it was so wrong and sinful, why did God respond? Others have imitated Gideon in this action.

They say: *Lord, if you want me to take this job, let me get a phone call from them today.*

But we must be careful. When Satan asked Jesus to "test" God by asking for a "sign," Jesus rebuked him (Matthew 4:5-7). So what is going on here?

Gideon was very specifically asking God to show him that he was not one of the forces of nature (like the other gods), but was sovereign over the forces of nature. Gideon, then, was not looking for "little signs" to help him make a decision. He was really seeking to understand the nature of God. We have to remember that he did not have the Bible, nor many of the "means of grace" that we have now (the word, baptism and the Lord's Supper, Christian fellowship). He was very specifically addressing the places where his faith was weak and uninformed.

We cannot use this as a justification to ask for little signs and signals. Gideon was not doing so—he was asking for supernatural revelation from God to show him who he really is. This therefore is not about how to make a decision. This is about how we need to ask God to give us a big picture of who he is. Living in the period of history we do, we have the advantage over Gideon of knowing Jesus Christ, the Son of God, as he reveals himself in his word: "In the past [including the time of Gideon] God spoke to our forefathers through the prophets at many times *and in various ways,* but in these last days he has spoken to us by his Son" (Hebrews 1:1-2).

> The fleece is about how we need to ask God to give us a big picture of who he is.

Gideon's request was for help to build up his faith. God, in his grace, responded (twice!). When we make the same request, God graciously responds: by pointing us to the fullest, final revelation of his character and his purposes—the Lord Jesus. When we, like Gideon, find ourselves doubting God's promises, or God's presence, we can ask him to point us again to his Son, saying: "I do believe; help me overcome my unbelief!" (Mark 9:24). This is what Gideon needed, and received. God will do the same for us.

Questions for reflection

1. What troubles are you facing? Will you see them as problems which need removing, or possible ways for God to change you and grow you?

2. What are the false gods which are demanding that you worship them alongside the one true God?

3. Are there parts of your life where you need to ask God to point you to his Son so that you can trust more fully in his promises?

6. GIDEON: TRIUMPH IN WEAKNESS

Boasting—encouraging others, and our own hearts, to give us glory—is opposed to, and saps, true faith. Conceit—being hungry for honor and glory—is the cousin of boasting. And before the Spirit-clothed Gideon, chosen by God to lead and save Israel, goes into battle, God wants to teach him and the rest of his people who deserves glory for salvation. It's a lesson we still need continually to learn as his people today.

You Need Fewer Men

The two armies—Gideon's men, and the Midianites who have terrorised Israel for seven years (6:1)—are camped close to one another (**7:1**). Battle cannot be far away, and at this point we are meant to assume that Israel will need every man if the enemy is to be defeated.

And yet God wants Gideon to have fewer men, not more! "You have too many men for me to deliver Midian into their hands" (**v 2**). This is not advice included in any military manual! Why does he want to reduce the army's strength?

"In order that Israel may not boast against me that her own strength has saved her" (**v 2**). God's people will either praise him for this victory; or they will praise—boast in—themselves. Gideon will either give the honor to his LORD, or he will seek it himself. Human nature is such that, if there is the tiniest opportunity to boast in our own work, we will. Notice that God says that any such boasting is "against me." As soon as we begin to believe that we deserve credit for rescuing or delivering ourselves, we take away glory from God that he deserves. We set up ourselves as alternative saviors. This is the greatest spiritual danger there is—that we should believe that we can save, or have saved, ourselves. The lesson we always need to learn is that salvation is by God's gracious action, not by earning it with our actions.

> The lesson we always need to learn is that salvation is by God's action, not ours.

God does not reduce the size of the army simply so that he can work through them to win victory. He can win victory through one man (as he will through Samson), or through thousands (as he did through Deborah and Barak's armies). God reduces the number of soldiers because he knows that the men are "too many" for Israel to see clearly where the praise and glory should go for the victory that will come.

And so God tells Gideon to decrease the numbers fighting for him in two ways. The first group which is sent home are those "who tremble with fear" (**v 3**). This was 22,000 men out of the 32,000—over two thirds! These were people who were able to admit publicly that they had no heart for battle. When Gideon, in obedience to God, offered to release anyone who was afraid to fight, it was a good psychological screening device. Clearly, there were many who were very frightened of battle but were unwilling to admit it. Those who were willing to admit their fear in public would also be far more likely to retreat in battle.

The reason it was good to send them home is a practical one. Fear is contagious, as we can often see in Judges. When any significant body of soldiers panic and flee, it can sap the determination of everyone and lead to a rout. Though it was surely discouraging to lose these numbers, it was still very practical to let them go. This move was concerned for the morale of the army. God's command and human logic line up here.

But that is not the case with the second group, who are sent home for much more obscure reasons. "There are still too many men" (**v 4**), the LORD tells Gideon. He must "take them down to the water, and I will sift them for you there" (**v 4**). Gideon must follow God's selection completely. Again, Gideon obeys, separating the 9,700 who knelt down to put their mouths to the water to drink from the 300 who used their hands to scoop up water (**v 5-6**).

And it is only the 300 who lapped who are to remain. With these few men "I will save you and give the Midianites into your hands" (**v 7**). "So Gideon sent the rest of the Israelites to their tents but kept the three hundred" (**v 8**). He had started the day with 32,000 men at his back. Now there are 300—a reduction of over 99%! Notice what great faith Gideon shows in verses 3-8, trusting God and not numbers. This is the faith for which he is commended in Hebrews 11:32-34: "I do not have time to tell [fully] about Gideon … who through faith conquered kingdoms … whose weakness was turned to strength; and who became powerful in battle and routed foreign armies."

People have differed over why God set the "drinking" test. It is typical for people to conclude that the 300 were being more alert and watchful. It is often assumed that they held on to their weapons and stayed on their feet while the others drank in such a way that they were defenseless. But this is a stretch. The text does not say anything about holding on to weapons. The first reduction may be about the quality of the fighting men—the second is not.

What the text does say, of course, is Judges **7:2**—that ultimately, both reductions are done "in order that Israel may not boast against me that her own strength has saved her." Gideon should look back and think: *This victory was God's, not mine. My only part was to trust and obey him. The glory is his, and the privilege is mine.* And the 300 men should likewise say

> Gideon should think: *This victory was God's. My only part was to trust and obey.*

after the battle: *It was impossible for us to win, few as we were—this victory must have been given by God. The glory is his, and the privilege is ours, for being allowed to be part of what he was doing.* And the rest of Israel should think: *I wasn't even there! God rescued me without me doing anything. Praise him!*

Again we see the principle of salvation that comes continually in Judges, and the rest of the Bible. God does not save through expected means, or through strength. Most of the judges are unlikely, and the victories defy the world's logic. Gideon is a man from a weak family in a weak tribe, and he must face the Midianites with only a handful of men.

My Weakness, His Strength

Another way to put this principle is found in 2 Corinthians 12:7-9. Paul has been privileged with a vision of heaven (v 2-6), yet has suffered from what he calls "a thorn in my flesh, a messenger of Satan, to torment me" (v 7). Paul had "pleaded with the Lord to take it away from me"—but instead he has taken away Paul's physical health by leaving this "thorn." Why? "To keep me from becoming conceited," so that he will not be hungry for his own honor, boasting about his own strength. Instead, he learns what God wants Gideon to learn—that "my grace is sufficient for you, for my power is made perfect [that is, most clearly revealed] in weakness" (v 9).

Paul's response is one of absolute trust, of the humility that is the opposite of conceit: "Therefore I will boast all the more gladly about my weaknesses, so that Christ's power may rest on me … when I am weak, then I am strong" (v 9-10). In other words, Paul says: *Look at how weak I am. All that has been achieved has been achieved by God. Look how strong he is to be able to work through **me**! Praise him!*

God does not simply work *in spite* of our weakness, but *because* of it. He says that his saving power does not work when we are strong or think we are strong—but rather, when we are weak, and know we are.

How does this work practically? First, this principle is the basis for salvation itself. We cannot be saved if we think we are good or able. God's saving power only works on us when we admit that we have no worthiness or goodness in ourselves.

Second, this principle explains how repentance works. **Paradoxically**, it is only as we repent and sorrow over our failures before God—only as we know our own weakness—that his love and grace become more precious and real to us. If someone says to you: *I paid one of your monthly bills*, you don't know how overjoyed to be until you hear how big the bill was. The bigger you understand your debts to be, the greater your joy in their payment will be. So it is only as we see our weakness that the strength of knowing God's grace and love comes. As the Lord Jesus pointed out, someone who thinks there is little in them to forgive will have little love for their Forgiver (Luke 7:47).

> It is only as we know our own weakness that God's love becomes more precious to us.

Third, this principle explains how we almost always grow as Christians. Our problems come because good things have become too important to us. Anger, fear or discouragement come because of "idols" —good things have become things we feel (at an emotional level) will really save us and give us worth. It is only when these things are threatened or removed that we turn and find our safety and significance in the Lord. That makes us stable and deep. This principle is perfectly mirrored here in this story. Gideon and all Israel were going to be tempted to put their confidence in their fighting men, but God removes virtually all of them so that the victory will lead them to trust in God in new ways. As they prepare for battle against the Midianite hordes, and look around them at 300 other men, they will surely feel extremely weak! How will they go into battle? Only if they know that they *are* weak, and yet that God is stronger than the largest army.

Questions for reflection

1. Have there been times in your life when God has weakened you so that you can see more clearly that he is the one who saves? How does this move you to praise him?

2. Have there been times when God has weakened you and then worked through your weakness? How does this move you to praise him?

3. How often do you spend time sorrowing over your sin, so that you can appreciate more fully God's forgiveness? How does doing this move you to love him?

PART TWO

The Loaf of Barley

Surely now it is time for the 300 to go into battle?! Not quite. God again speaks to Gideon—but this time the purpose is not to remove his potential for self-boasting, but to give him assurance of victory.

Again, God tells Gideon: "I am going to give [Midian] into your hands" (Judges **7:9**). But, with wonderful thoughtfulness, the King of the universe says: "If you are afraid to attack, go down to the camp ... and listen to what they are saying. Afterward, you will be encouraged to attack" (**v 10-11**).

At first sight, what greets Gideon is terrifying! The Midianites and their allies are "thick as **locusts**." And their camels—the beasts which they have used to subjugate Israel—can "no more be counted than the sand on the seashore" (**v 12**). How will this encourage Gideon to attack with 300 men?!

Because God has sent him to the camp "just as a man was telling a friend his dream" (**v 13**), where a loaf of barley struck a Midianite tent with such force that it collapsed. This is, of course, most unlikely—no one worries that a loaf of bread might take down their tent, just as the Midianites would not have been overly concerned about 32,000 men from a nation they had terrorized for eight years. Yet this is the content of the dream; and so "his friend responded, 'This can be nothing other than the sword of Gideon son of Joash, the Israelite. God has given the Midianites and the whole camp into his hands'" (**v 14**).

When we know we are weak, we need to remember that God is strong. We also need to be reminded of the truth that those things which stand opposed to us are not as strong as they often appear. Satan cannot force us to sin; the power of idols can be broken; those who mock or

Things which stand opposed to us are not as strong as they often appear.

persecute us are often conflicted and broken beneath their confident exterior. God graciously gives Gideon the opportunity to see this: that this vast army, "thick as locusts," underneath their armour have trembling hearts. They know what Gideon is only now convinced of: "God has given the Midianites … into [Gideon's] hands."

The God who Reassures

Gideon's response is to worship God (**v 15**). God has gone ahead of him in every way. All he can do is praise him. His trust in God to give victory spurs him into action: "he returned to the camp of Israel and called out, 'Get up! The LORD has given the Midianite camp into your hands" (**v 15**).

What does this incident tell us about our Christian lives? First, that God is the great Reassurer. He is the one who takes initiative here. Gideon needs this visit to the quaking enemy camp in order to get him to worship, trust and attack—but he does not ask for it.

God goes out of his way to reassure his people. The whole book of 1 John, for instance, is written to assure us that we "know that we have come to know him" (1 John 2:3). The Holy Spirit works in us to assure us that we are God's children (Romans 8:16). A good husband reminds his wife: *I love you, and I'm here for you* and particularly reassures her of this in difficult times, never saying: *I told you I was committed to you on our wedding day. You should know I love you!* If you love someone, you are willing to assure them of your love—and God is the same.

Notice, though, that God may ask us to take risks on the way to assurance. Going into the enemy camp is dangerous for Gideon and his servant. But it is the place where God gives him confidence, leads him to worship, and stirs him to action. God often gives us what we need as we do what he has asked us to do. Jesus commanded his disciples to "go and make disciples of all nations" (Matthew 28:19), and *then* promised: "I am with you always." Paul worked hard to be able to bring his churches to maturity: "To this end I labor," he wrote, working long and hard himself, often struggling, and as he did so finding "all [God's] energy, which so powerfully works in me" (Colossians 1:29). We can find that we lack assurance of God's presence with us and power for us because we never take a risk and do something bold in obedience to him—we never step out in faith and find him there.

We, like Gideon, are in repeated need of assurance. He cannot sustain his direction of energy without repeated lessons and lots of confirmation of God's presence, guidance and power. When we see the narrative "telescoped" as it is, the impression is that Gideon is very weak. He needed the angel to burn up his offering, two miraculous fleece episodes, *and* this Midianite dream and its interpretation, before he would attack! But if we think of our own spiritual history, we will see the same thing. We often think: *I'll never forget or doubt God again*—and then very soon become indifferent or anxious once more. How many resolutions to live radically for God have we made that we have not kept? We aren't any different from Gideon. We rarely relax and trust him. No matter what God does for us, our hearts are quite stubborn and find it very hard joyfully and confidently to trust and live by his promises.

> We can find we lack assurance because we never step out in faith and find God there.

We need God's ongoing assurance and reminder that he is with us and for us. How does God assure us? First, he assures us through his word—directly to Gideon (Judges **7:9-11**), through his inspired Scriptures to us. When we read his word and especially his promises, we often find that the Holy Spirit comes and makes the promises both real and sweet to us.

Second, God often assures us through other people. Here, God does not give Gideon his promise directly. Rather, he gives it through the mouth of another. It is important to have others who are close friends who can do this: people we spend time with and allow to encourage us about who we are as God's children, and where we and our world are headed (Hebrews 10:25).

Third, God often assures us through circumstances of life, as here. In a sense, Gideon just happens to be at the right place at the right time to hear this conversation. But of course, this is not a coincidence. God has brought him to this place to hear these words to find reassurance.

How do we know we have been reassured? Judges **7:15** shows us—it is at any time when we have been led to heartfelt praise and worship of God, and radical, confident obedience to him.

The Mighty Warrior

Gideon's new-found confidence leads him into battle. He comes up with his battle plan, dividing his tiny army into three groups and equipping them with trumpets and torches hidden inside jars (**v 16**). Reaching the camp at the changing of the guard (**v 19**), they blow their trumpets, break their jars to reveal their lights, and shout (**v 19-20**).

It is a brilliant plan. First, it negates the size disparity between the armies. The Israelites appear and sound far greater in size than they really are.

Second, it negates the difference in strength. It makes the camels a non-factor (in fact, they may have increased the confusion and mayhem in the camp).

Third, it takes advantage of the time when the enemy are weakest. The night was probably divided into three watches of four hours each, a third of the army taking each watch. At the changing of the guard, one third of the army would have been walking back to their tents, while another third would have been asleep. So, when those who were asleep heard the noise and rushed out of their tents, they would have discovered their camp full of armed men walking towards them. In the dark, the truth that they were fellow Midianites would have been unclear until it was too late.

In many ways, this strategy was Gideon's. He is indeed a "mighty warrior" after all, just as God had said (6:12). Yet truly, this tactic was God's. After all, Gideon would never have chosen 300 men from 32,000 if God hadn't told him to. And Gideon would never have known of the spirit of nervousness among the numerous Midianites if God had not told him to visit their camp. God gives us gifts to use in his service, such as Gideon's previously unseen military genius. But he also gives us the circumstances which allow us to use them. Even in our successes, we can, and should, praise God for giving us both the means and opportunity to be successful.

> Even in successes, we can praise God for the means and opportunity.

Victory

The outcome of the battle, of course, is a foregone conclusion, since God has already announced its result (6:16; 7:7). Gideon's plan works perfectly; all the Israelites need do is hold their position. "All the Midianites ran, crying out as they fled. When the three hundred trumpets sounded, the LORD caused the men throughout the camp to turn on each other with their swords. The army fled…" (**v 21-22**). In the end, even the three hundred kill no enemy soldiers! None of them could return home singing of what they had done, but only of what the LORD had done as they watched.

The victory is made complete as the Midianites run, pursued by Israel (**v 23**), only to discover when they reach the eastern border of the country that Gideon has arranged the tribe of Ephraim to form a welcome party on the River Jordan (**v 24**).

There is a wonderful circularity to this section of the Gideon narrative. We first met him sheltering from the Midianites in a winepress (6:11). The first reassurance of God's presence with him took place at a rock, when the angel of the LORD burned up his offering. Now, the kings of the enemies God used Gideon to defeat are killed at a rock and at a winepress (**7:25**). The enemies of God's people are truly not as strong as they may appear!

Questions for reflection

1. How does it encourage you today to remember that the things that oppose your faith and obedience may be stronger than you, but they are not stronger than God?

2. In what ways are you being challenged to step out in faith, finding God's strength and reassurance as you do so?

3. What gifts has God given you to serve him with? What circumstances has he given you in which to use those gifts?

7. GIDEON AND ABIMELECH: RULING AS KINGS

With the previous judges, once God has rescued his people from op-pression to idols and to enemies, the only further detail given is the length of the peace they enjoyed under that judge's leadership. With Gideon, it's not so simple. Israel is on a general downward spiral. And we see two things for the first time in the career of Gideon: the peo-ple beginning to "back-slide" during, rather than after, the rule of a judge-savior; and there are deep flaws in the judge-savior's rule. So rather than summing up Gideon's post-victory leadership in a verse, the writer of the book devotes two chapters to it.

Teaching a Lesson

Ephraim is one of the more powerful tribes in Israel, and Gideon had called them out to help him cut off the fleeing Midianites (7:24-25). But the Ephraimites are unhappy with him: "Why didn't you call us when you went to fight Midian?" (**8:1**) In fact, it's unlikely that they would have been willing to march under Gideon's command: they were one of the strongest tribes, economically and militarily, and he was from the weakest clan in the tribe of Manasseh (6:15).

Their criticism here is born of frustration at having missed out on the glory of the victory. Ironically, it reveals two truths: first, that God was absolutely correct to say that Israel would want to "boast against" him and glorify themselves in victory; second, that Ephraim would not have respected or deferred to God's chosen judge.

Gideon's response to them is respectful and diplomatic. He points out how much more powerful their tribe is than his clan (**8:2**)—and that they (unlike him) have already captured and killed two Midianite leaders (**v 3**). Ephraim's snub and scolding must have been hard to take, but he holds his tongue—and, with their desire for glory and praise satisfied, "their resentment against him subsided" (**v 3**).

We might want, at this point, to praise Gideon for his humility and peacefulness—but the next section shows that these were not what drove his diplomacy toward Ephraim. Exhausted from the pursuit of the Midianite kings Zebah and Zalmunna (**v 4**), Gideon asks the people of the town of Succoth to feed his men. But they refuse to help (**v 5**). Like the Ephraimites, they show a complete lack of gratitude to Gideon for defeating their enemy. Essentially, they say to him: *Do you have these Midianite kings in your hands yet? No? Then don't look to us for help!* They know that if Gideon isn't able to catch and kill their leaders, then the Midianites will regroup and return—and any towns who helped Gideon will be destroyed. Ephraim was annoyed Gideon hadn't called them out earlier—Succoth would rather he hadn't called on them till later! And, as Gideon moves on with his men, he finds the same response from Peniel (**v 8**).

> Humility was not what drove Gideon's diplomacy.

Gideon answers Succoth and Peniel very differently from Ephraim. "When the Lord has given Zebah and Zalmunna into my hand, I will tear your flesh with desert thorns and briers ... When I return in triumph, I will tear down this tower" (**v 7, 9**).

This reveals that Gideon's diplomacy regarding Ephraim was not because he did not want to strike at them, but because he could not. And it reveals that, despite God making sure that the victory was so miraculous that everyone should have seen that it was given by God, not earned by Gideon, Gideon himself has forgotten "the lesson of the 300." He feels that he ought to receive admiration and honor for what he has done. Gideon's anger at the people of Succoth and Peniel shows that he expects to be given glory for his achievements (which he is forgetting were, in fact, God's). When Succoth and Peniel fail to trust that Gideon will

> Gideon's anger shows he expects to be given glory.

triumph over Midian, he does not say to them: *Yes, I know it is hard to believe we can beat them. But God in his grace is using us to win the battle, so don't trust my strength, but do trust in his.* Instead, he says: *You dare to doubt **me**? I'll show you my power when I get back. You'll learn to have respect for me.*

And so, when he has returned from again routing a far stronger force with his three hundred men, and capturing Zebah and Zalmanna (**v 10-12**), Gideon is as good as his word. He seizes a member of his own people, Israel (**v 14**), discovers the names of the elders of Succoth, reminds them that "you taunted me" (**v 15**), and then "taught the men of Succoth a lesson by punishing them with desert thorns and briers" (**v 16**). In Peniel, things are even worse—he "pulled down the tower … and killed the men of the town" (**v 17**).

Verses 18-19 add a new detail to the narrative: that the Midianite kings had killed Gideon's own brothers, and that their deaths are what have made him so determined to catch them. Gideon's ruthless, remarkable pursuit has been motivated less by a desire to complete the deliverance of God's people than by a drive for personal vengeance— for the honor of his own family. This is why Gideon asks "Jether, his oldest son" to "kill them" (**v 20**)—he wants to humiliate these kings by having them killed by a mere boy. In the end, Gideon performs the execution himself (**v 21**), and with their deaths, victory is complete. But its manner points to a future under Gideon which will not be marked by real peace.

The Danger of Success

Gideon's need for respect and honor—and his violent, bitter rage when he fails to be given what he thinks he deserves—shows that his success in battle has been the worst thing for him. He has become addicted to and dependent on his success.

There is a terrible spiritual danger involved in the receiving of any blessing. Success can easily cause us to forget God's grace, because our hearts are desperate to believe that we can save ourselves. God-given victory can easily be used to confirm the belief that, in fact, we have earned blessing for ourselves, and should receive the praise and glory for that success.

For example, imagine a man who works extremely hard at his job because he needs to prove himself through financial success. What is the worst thing that can happen to him? The obvious answer is *career failure*. Of course, someone who is basing their happiness and identity on their work will be devastated by career failure. But at least, through the failure, he may stop idolizing career advancement. He may realize that status and money could never fulfill him. No, the worst thing that can happen to him is *career success*. Success will only confirm his belief that he can fulfill himself and control his own life. He will be more a slave to success and money than if he failed. He will feel proud and superior to others. He will expect deference and "bowing and scraping" from others.

Back in 7:15, when Gideon knew his own weakness and understood that victory could only be by grace, he worshiped and honored God. But that is the last time we see him doing that. Now, he worships success and the honor it will bring him. He has entirely forgotten who it is that called him, equipped him, reassured him, and won the battle for him. We, too, find it all too easy to forget that everything about our salvation, and all of our good works, are gifts of grace, not of our own success—that "it is by grace you have been saved, through faith—and this not from yourselves, it is the gift of God—not by works, so that no one can boast. For we are God's workmanship, created in Christ Jesus to do good works, which God prepared in advance for us to do" (Ephesians 2:8-10). We need to remember that we are saved by grace when we fail. But we need to remember it much more when we succeed.

King Gideon?

Now Israel ask Gideon to be a king: "Rule over us—you, your son and your grandson—because you have saved us" (**Judges 8:22**). Just as Gideon has begun to forget who it was who gave victory over Midian, so have the rest of Israel. *Gideon, you should be our king because you beat Midian,* is their reasoning.

Israel wants to reject God's method of ruling his people. A judge is anointed by him, to deal with the crisis at hand and to lead the people back to living under his rule. But if Gideon says "yes," Israel will have a king appointed by humans, and rule will pass on down to others automatically.

Gideon **discerns** the underlying motive for asking for a king—they want to be ruled by a man, not by God (**v 23**). With a king, they would not need to look to God for salvation, and wait for him to send them a savior. The desire for a king is actually another effort at self-salvation. Gideon turns down their request: "I will not rule over you ... the LORD will rule over you" (**v 23**). They don't need a king to obey; they need to obey the King they have!

Verse 23 is really the last time that Gideon remembers who God is and who he is. Ironically and tragically, he almost immediately contradicts what he has just said. He has refused to be their king, because that position and honor belong to God alone—but then he starts to assume the honor due to a king. He asks for a financial reward for their deliverance (**v 24**), and becomes a very rich man (**v 25-26**—there are echoes of Israel making a golden calf to worship at the foot of Mount Sinai on the way to the promised land, see Exodus 32:1-4). Then "Gideon made the gold into an ephod, which he placed in Ophrah, his town" (Judges **8:27**).

What is going on here? The ephod was worn by the **high priest** in the tabernacle, the tent where God was present among his people, which at this point was sited in Shiloh (18:31). On its front were the Urim and Thummim—two stones that were used to receive "yes' or "no" answers from God (they may have been like coins, which were flipped; likely, two upsides meant "yes," two downsides meant "no," one of each meant "no answer"). The ephod designated the true place of God's dwelling, and was a way to discern God's will in times of crisis.

In making his own copy, Gideon essentially sets up his home town as a rival place of worship. He wants to encourage people to come to him for guidance, to see his home town as the place where God can be found. Gideon has used God to consolidate his own position, instead of using his position to serve and be used by God.

What effect does this have? **8:27**—"All Israel prostituted themselves by worshiping it there." The judge is supposed to turn people from unfaithfulness to the true God. Gideon leads them into it.

It is only at this point that we are told that "during Gideon's lifetime, the land enjoyed peace forty years" (**v 28**). But we know by now that this is a compromised peace. It is peace without worship, and peace without obedience.

And Gideon continues to act more and more like a king. His family arrangements—he has seventy sons by many wives, and one by a **concubine** (**v 29-31**)—are those of someone aspiring to kingship. He even calls his illegitimate son "Abimelech" (**v 31**), which means *My father is king*! What Gideon has rejected in name, he then lives out in reality.

> What Gideon has rejected in name, he lives out in reality.

Yet all this is only a few verses since Gideon turned down the kingship because "the LORD will rule over you"! How could Gideon refuse to become a king because he knows God is the King, and then act like one? Quite simply, he knew something intellectually which had not really gripped his heart. He had a mental grasp of the doctrine of God's grace and rule, and he could give the right answer in some situations. But his heart had not really understood how this truth worked itself out in all of life. There was a huge and growing gap between what he believed about God in his head, and the motives of his heart and the actions of his hands. Gideon's mistake was a failure to live out what he knew to be true—what Paul in Galatians 2:14 called a failure to (literally) "walk in line with the gospel."

The nineteenth-century preacher, C.H. Spurgeon, once warned younger Christians: "Don't go into the ministry to save your soul." He knew it is very easy for us to use church leadership not to serve and honor God, but to win influence and honor for ourselves. Of course, Gideon-like, we still say that God is King; but we want people to look to *us* for guidance, for answers, for salvation. We need to be needed. We make an ephod and wear it ourselves. How subtle. How deadly.

> It is very easy to use church leadership not to serve and honor God, but to win influence and honor for ourselves.

And how wonderful to look at the One each judge is a shadow of and see how he used his position. Unlike Gideon, he had every right to demand service as a King. Unlike Gideon, he *is* the tabernacle, God's ultimate dwelling-place on earth. Yet Jesus resisted the temptation to rule in power over the nations (Luke 4:5-8), because he "did not come to be served, but to serve, and to give his life as a ransom for many" (Mark 10:45). He has **ransomed** us from our self-honoring reactions to success, and our self-hating responses to failure. He used his position as the Son of God to give us freedom from needing respect or being crushed by lack of it. Unlike the ephod, here is the One to whom we rightly should come in worship.

Questions for reflection

1. Are there aspects of your life and work you think you should get more recognition and honor for? How will the gospel of grace help you deal well with your successes?

2. In which areas of your life do you need to walk more closely, or clearly, in line with the gospel?

3. How does looking at the servant-heartedness of our Savior liberate us from seeing ministry as self-salvation?

PART TWO

The Son of Gideon

Until this chapter, there has been a familiar sequence of events. Sin, oppression, crying out, a judge raised up, victory, peace. But now, we have a complete departure from the sequence. It is a horrendous episode in Israel's history.

Abimelech is Gideon's son by his concubine, who lived in Shechem (**8:31**). This means that from his birth, he had been an outsider in his own family. Unlike Gideon's other seventy sons, he was illegitimate. He did not stand to inherit. As the story unfolds, we see a man who feels that whatever he will get out of life, he will have to get for himself—and who is utterly determined to get whatever he can.

The scene of most of the action is important. As Gettysburg and Montgomery are places of great historical and national significance for Americans, so Shechem was a place of huge importance in Israel. It was the place where God appeared to **Abram** to tell him that *this* was the land he had promised to give him, and so it was the first place in the promised land to have an altar built in worship of the Lord (Genesis 12:6-7). And it was the first place where Abram's descendants gathered to worship the Lord after they had crossed into the land under Joshua (Joshua 8:30-35—Shechem sat at the foot of the two mountains mentioned here). Historically, then, it is the spiritual center and thermometer of Israel. What happens in Shechem in Judges 9 would be similar to Americans deciding to reinstitute slavery at a meeting in Gettysburg or racial segregation at Montgomery.

Grasping Power

Every other leader in Judges is called by God without seeking the role. Abimelech grasps it for himself, going to his mother's brothers in Shechem (Judges **9:1**) and pointing out that he is a son of his kinglike father *and* a kinsmen of theirs (**v 2**). His argument is: *Wouldn't it be* better to have just one ruler? And wouldn't it be good to ensure that that ruler is one of us? Wouldn't it be good if your king were me?

The men of Shechem agree (**v 3**). So "they gave him seventy shekels of silver from the temple of Baal-Berith, and Abimelech used it to hire reckless adventurers, who became his followers" (**v 4**). His rise to power is facilitated not by obedience to the LORD, but by a false god's funds. And it will be founded on the blood of his half-brothers, 70 of whom he kills in cold blood "on one stone" (**v 5**). Gideon killed fellow Israelites; now Abimelech murders his own family.

The other leaders in this book govern on the basis of some revelation from God. But here authority is not a matter of judging or delivering, but rather is an exercise of naked power. Unlike his father, Abimelech makes no pretence not to be a king (**v 6**), nor to be ruling in obedience to God.

There is a good lesson in choosing a leader here. We are often far too easily impressed by qualities that are unimportant to God. Further, we can far too easily be swayed by **pragmatic** arguments. God does not prize popularity, humor, or academic intelligence, being an extrovert, and so on. He seeks men who hold to his truth, seek to lead their family rightly, are patient and self-controlled (1 Timothy 3:1-7; Titus 1:6-9). He does not want well-mannered, well-dressed, 21st-century equivalents of Abimelech, chosen for the wrong reasons and the wrong qualities.

> God does not prize popularity, or humor, or intelligence.

The Thornbush King

Only one half-brother escapes—Jotham. While Abimelech means *My father is king*, Jotham means *Yahweh (ie: the LORD) is perfect/blameless*. So as Jotham calls out to the men of Shechem, there is a battle for hearts and minds between human self-reliant power (Abimelech) and reliance on and worship of the LORD (Jotham).

The story Jotham tells in Judges **9:8-14** is designed to show the ridiculousness of choosing Abimelech as king. Olive trees (**v 8-9**), fig-trees (**10-11**) and vines (**v 12-13**) were valuable, and produced the main crops of the Israelite agricultural economy. But they pass on becoming king. "Finally all the trees said to the thornbush, 'Come and be our king'" (**v 14**). Thornbushes were not at all valuable plants. They were too short and scraggy to provide any shade from the heat, and often caught fire, which spread to surrounding foliage and destroyed more valuable trees. The thornbush points this out in agreeing to become king (**v 15**), and makes the remarkable claim (given it only grows a foot or two off the ground) that other trees can "come and take refuge in my shade."

What is Jotham's point? **Verses 16-20** explain it. Essentially, he says: *If you've been fair to Gideon's family in making Abimelech your king (and let's face it, you haven't, but if you have), then may you find great blessing in the rule of King Abimelech. But if you haven't (and, let's face it, you haven't), then I hope you and he get what you all deserve—you burned by him, and he burned by you.*

The Fire of the Thornbush

What follows certainly constitutes a raging fire. The citizens of Shechem have already shown themselves prone to switch their loyalty, and when "Gaal son of Ebed" moves into Shechem, they "put their confidence in him (**v 26**). There's great irony in the fact that Gaal worships at the temple of the idol whose funds Abimelech had used (**v 27**, see v 4), and uses the same arguments as Abimelech had (**v 28-29**, see v 2).

Abimelech, unlike the Shechemites, is fiercely loyal—to his own cause. His father, Gideon, had ended up driven by personal vengeance and a thirst for the honor he felt he deserved. The son takes that quest to new heights. He fights Gaal (**v 30-41**), conquers Shechem (**v 42-44**), and then "captured it and killed its people" (**v 45**). The place where Abram had worshiped the LORD, and where Joshua and all the people had worshiped him, ends up barren, salt scattered over it so that its fields cannot grow crops (**v 45**).

Over a thousand Shechemites take refuge in the temple of their idol, in the stronghold of the tower (**v 46**), but Abimelech's thirst for revenge is not sated. He leads his men to burn it down (**v 48-49**). "So all the people in the tower of Shechem, about a thousand men and women, also died" (**v 49**). It looks as though the town of Thebez will suffer the same fate (**v 50-52**). But as Abimelech "approached the entrance to the tower to set it on fire, a woman dropped an upper **millstone** on his head and cracked his skull" (**v 53**). Fatally injured, Abimelech (ever mindful of his reputation) has his servant run him through so that a woman won't have killed him (**v 54**).

Is God Absent?

Between 8:34 and 10:6 God is not mentioned at all by his personal covenant name, the LORD. This is a picture of a society and ruler who desire to push God out of the picture completely—unworshiped, and unconsidered.

So is God absent? As the Shechemites use idol-money to fund a massacre, and as Abimelech works his bloody way around Israel, God seems absent. As Jotham sat in Beer, "afraid of his brother Abimelech" (**9:21**), he could be forgiven for wondering if his curse of **verses 16-20** had been mistaken. When the Shechemites and Abimelech himself lie prone by the end of chapter 9, it has been as a result of a vengeful feud and a fortunate throw by a woman. God does seem absent.

But in verses **23-24** and **56-57**, the narrator lifts the curtain of human affairs to show us a glimpse of what God was doing. "God sent an evil spirit between Abimelech and the citizens of Shechem … in order that the crime against Jerub-Baal's seventy sons, the shedding of their blood, might be avenged" (**v 23-24**). Once Abimelech is dead, he comments: "Thus God repaid the wickedness that Abimelech had done … God also made the men of Shechem pay for all their wickedness" (**v 56-57**).

God may have been silent, but he was not absent. In what seemed like the natural course of events, he was acting in judgment. There was no lightning bolt from heaven... but there was justice. As Paul puts it in Romans 1:18: "The wrath of God *is being* revealed from heaven against all the godlessness and wickedness of men who suppress the truth by their wickedness." God's judgment is not only reserved for a future day; it is a present reality.

This horrific episode in Judges points us to three truths about God's present judgment:

- It comes unseen. The people at the time could not have seen the spirit God sent to use the evil in Shechemite hearts for his just purposes. And in our own day, we have no divinely inspired narrator to lift the curtain to tell us where, when and how God is judging people. We know it is happening; but we can never point to any one event and say: *God is judging you for this particular sin you have committed.*

- It comes after a wait. Three years passed between Jotham warning of judgment and judgment coming (**v 22-23**), three years in which Abimelech ruled and in which his crimes seemed to have paid. The wait is covered in a single verse in the narrative; to Jotham, those three years must have seemed considerably longer! He had to learn patience and trust.

- It comes through the outworking of human sin. Shechem was destroyed because of its disloyalty. Its greatest sin was its downfall. Abimelech was destroyed because of his desire to maintain his position at any human cost. He had no need to attack Thebez. His greatest sin was also his downfall. God in his judgment uses the tools of human rebellion against those who rebel.

> God in his judgment uses the tools of human rebellion against those who rebel.

Grace Beyond Terror

In the rule of Abimelech, Israel plumbs new depths. Yet there is more to come "after the time of Abimelech" (Judges **10:1**). "Tola … rose to save Israel" (**v 1**). He "led Israel twenty-three years" (**v 2**). This is the same language used of Deborah, one of the best of the judges. God has raised up someone else who saved and led Israel in the way she did. And he is followed by another twenty-two years of peace under Jair (**v 3**).

This is the sheer grace of God. The people have completely abandoned him. They have opted to be led by a man who was chosen not by the LORD, but by himself, who was recommended not by the LORD's divine commission but by his own power. Israel have sunk to the depths and they are not even crying out in repentance, yet God sends them Tola and Jair to be the judge-saviors they are not asking for.

But unlike the earlier non-cyclical judge, Shamgar, no enemy is named (3:31). Who did Tola rise to save Israel *from*? Chapter 9 gives the answer! Tola saved Israel *from itself*. God's people, ultimately, need a leader who will rescue us from ourselves—from the failings and ambitions of our own hearts, and from the divisions and strife among us. It is a great reminder that the church's greatest problem is the church! When we see churches with godly, humble leadership; with gospel-centered unity; which enjoy and pursue and share peace with justice and love—we, unlike Gideon and Abimelech, must give thanks to the God who has, in his grace, given us the Spirit to transform our hearts and restore our relationships.

> The church's greatest problem is the church!

Questions for reflection

1. What impresses you most in your church's leaders, both locally and nationally? Are you influenced more by God's priorities, or the world's?

2. How does the unseen reality of God's present judgment encourage and challenge your view of your life and this world?

3. How has God saved you from yourself? How does this make you feel about him?

8. JEPHTHAH: THE OUTCAST

Abimelech had oppressed his own idolatrous countrymen. Tola and Jair had risen to save Israel from themselves. But now, the familiar and depressing cycle begins once more. "Again" Israel worship idols— "The Baals and the Ashtoreths, and the gods of Aram, the gods of Sidon, the gods of Moab, the gods of the Ammonites and the gods of the Philistines" (**10:6**).

The Baals and the Ashtoreths were the gods of the "native" Canaanites. But the gods of Aram (to the north-west) and Sidon (to the north), or Ammon and Moab (to the east) and the Philistines (to the south), belonged to peoples outside of Canaan who often came into Canaan and oppressed the Israelites. Othniel helped Israel against the king of Aram (3:10), Ehud against the Moabites and Ammonites (3:12-13), Shamgar against the Philistines (3:31), and Deborah against the Canaanites (5:19).

In other words, every time Israel worshiped the idols of a nation, that nation ended up oppressing them. This time, Israel has added the gods of the Ammonites and Philistines—and in consequence, they are given over to being oppressed by the Ammonites and Philistines (**10:7**). Idolatry leads to enslavement.

It is interesting to notice that not only does idolatry lead to slavery, but slavery to idolatry. You would think that, once a nation was oppressing and enslaving Israel, Israel would absolutely hate the gods of that nation! But though the Ammonites had oppressed Israel in 3:13, here is Israel serving their gods, leading to enslavement to the Ammonites again. Despite their pain and misery, Israel continued to worship the same idols that let them down and brought them into trouble.

It is easy to see the futility of this in Israel, from our vantage point of a different era and culture. But human hearts have not changed. They still assure us that, when an idol leads to slavery, what we need is more of that idol. If someone seeks their value and purpose in a relationship—for example, sacrificing everything to a marriage which then fails—it seems very natural to think: *I need to find another relationship. I need a better spouse.* We see our problem not as worshiping an idol, but not worshiping an idol *enough*.

Sold

God, in his settled anger at idolatry, "sold them into the hands of" their enemies (**10:7**). This is a strong phrase. It has been used of what God did in Judges 2:14, 3:8, and 4:2, as well as here. When you sell a car to another person, it means the new owner can do with it as he pleases. When we look back at how God "sold" the Israelites before, we know this does not mean that he abandoned them or **nullified** his promises to them. It does mean, however, that he stopped protecting them in some way. He let the things they had been serving actually begin to dominate and "own" them.

Romans 1:23-25 is a fascinating parallel passage. There Paul talks about idolatry. He speaks of people who "exchanged the glory of … God for images made to look like mortal man and birds and animals and reptiles" (v 23). What was the result? "Therefore God gave them up in the lusts of their hearts" (v 24, ESV). The word "lusts" in Greek is *epithumia*, a word that means an overwhelming drive, an enslaving, uncontrollable desire. To "give up" means that God allows the things in which we hope instead of God to become ruling powers in our lives. Once God gave them over for worshiping idols, they "worshiped and served created things rather than the Creator" (v 25). The judgment for idolatry is… idolatry.

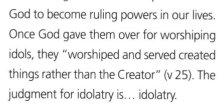

The judgment for idolatry is… idolatry.

Idolatry and slavery go hand in hand. Idolatry leads to slavery and slavery to idolatry. So God says to the person who worships money: *If you want to live for money instead of for me, then money will rule your life. It will control your heart and emotions. If you want to live for popularity instead of for me, then popular acclaim will rule and control you. If you want another god besides me—go ahead. Let's see how merciful it is to you, how effective it is in saving and guiding and enlightening you.*

I Will No Longer Save You

The oppression of Israel is the worst yet: total—they were "shattered" (Judges **10:8**); lengthy (eighteen years, **v 8**); universal, including all Israel on both sides of the Jordan (**v 8-9**). And so the Israelites cry out to the LORD, confessing: "We have sinned against you, forsaking our God and serving the Baals" (**v 10**).

God does not immediately forgive them and begin to answer their prayer. We also saw this in 6:7-10, where the people cried to God and in response he sent them a stern warning. Here, God's response is even more surprisingly harsh. He has saved them time and time again (**10:11-12**); and time and time again they have "forsaken [him] and served other gods"—and so, in a crushing line, God tells his people: "I will no longer save you" (**v 13**). He will not answer them—they should cry to the gods they have been worshiping (**v 14**).

Michael Wilcock explains why:

"The LORD … is saying, 'I know what this cry of yours is. It is merely a cry for help, which might just as well be addressed to the Baals as to me.'" (*The Message of Judges,* page 108)

When God says: "Go and cry out to the gods you have chosen" (**v 14**), he means that their request is simply the request of a weak party to a stronger one for the alleviation of their misery. They are saying: *OK, you have us over a barrel! We are in trouble because we broke your rules! Now help us please; get us out of trouble.* But repentance is heart-felt conviction and hatred of what was done, regardless of whether it caused trouble or not. In other words, they are sorry for the *consequences* of their sin, but they are not really sorry for the *sin*. It is possible to turn from idolatry in an idolatrous way—and that is what they are doing. They are treating God as if he were one of their idols. They are trying to push the right buttons, make the right sacrifices, in order to get him to exert his power for them.

> It is possible to turn from idolatry in an idolatrous way.

The Israelites understand the point. Their request in **verse 15** is different from the one of **verse 10**. Saying: *Do with us as you wish, though we still beg for mercy*, it shows a heart change. Before, they were focused completely on their condition and comfort. They were saying: *We are broken—fix us please!* But now they are willing to admit that God is under no obligation to fix them and take away their trouble. This means they are saying: *We want you, even if it means we are going to keep suffering (though we'd rather not).*

Why is that a sign of real faith? If we say to God: *I want you because I want/need you to give me "X,"* we reveal that "X" is our real, ultimate god. When we say: *I want you regardless of whether you give me X, Y, or Z*, then we are making the true God our God again.

Second, when they "got rid of the foreign gods" (**v 16**), they showed that they were going beneath the surface to change their hearts, not just their superficial behavior. Judges shows that the Israelites often changed their behavior in order to curry favor with the Lord, but they kept their idols in their homes, as "insurance." But repentance gets beneath the surface. It does not just focus on behavior but on motives.

The two signs of real repentance are:

- a sorrow for sin, rather than just for its consequences;
- a sorrow over idolatrous motives, not just behavioral change.

And God responds to his repentant, oppressed people with mercy: "he could bear Israel's misery no longer" (**v 16**). He will act to save Israel; even though he had said "I will no longer save you" (**v 13**). Again, we see the tension between God's holiness and his mercy, between the conditionality and the unconditionality of his promises to his people—a tension resolved fully only at the cross (see pages 26-28).

The Crime Boss

With the Ammonite and Israelite camps drawn up for battle (**v 17**), and the men of Gilead searching for the man who will lead them in battle and beyond (**v 18**), the scene is set for God's deliverer to arrive.

he is an unsurprising, and a surprising, choice (**11:1**)! Like Gideon, Jephthah is a "mighty warrior"—and similar to Gideon's son Abimelech, "his mother was a prostitute." In the world's eyes, leaders are people who have an Ivy League or Oxbridge pedigree, strong family background (and thus emotional health), and no police record! But Jephthah is someone without any of these things. He was the illegitimate son of a prostitute who was driven out of his home, probably as a very young person, by his half-brothers (**v 2**). So he came from (to say the least) a deeply dysfunctional family. Then, in the wilderness, he attracted a band of "outlaws," men who lived through robbery (**v 3**, NRSV). Jephthah was in organized crime; a kind of underworld boss, or (more romantically) a pirate. He was a complete outcast and a criminal from a broken home.

Yet God raises him up to be the savior. As the Ammonites "made war on Israel" (**v 4**), the Gilead leaders "went to get Jephthah," telling him to command their army so they could fight their enemy (**v 5-6**). Jephthah is not so easily won. "Didn't you hate me?" he points out (**v 7**). *You only want me now because you're in trouble.*

It is not enough for the Gileadites to use Jephthah, who they've treated so badly, to rescue them. They must also, as they realize, make him their head, too—their judge, who they will obey (**v 8**). Experience is the mother of caution, and Jephthah double checks they really mean what they say (**v 9**)! Reassured (**v 10**), he accepts the judgeship, and "the people made him head and commander over them" (**v 11**).

Many have noticed the similarity between the Israelites' dialogue with God in 10:10-16 and with Jephthah here. The Gileadites presume that Jephthah will help them. He makes them ask again, with more humility and with an acceptance that rescue comes with rule. This is exactly the same exchange that God had with Israel! We are seeing that God's people must learn that their treatment of God's judge is the way in which they are, in fact, treating God himself, for better or for worse. God's leaders are "types" who each point to his greatest Judge, the Lord Jesus. The way people treat Jesus is the way they are, in fact, treating God. You cannot respect God or truly repent without acknowledging the right to rule of Jesus. And you cannot have Jesus' rescue without accepting his rule.

> You cannot have Jesus' rescue without accepting his rule.

But Jephthah does not simply rise to be judge *despite* his rejection and suffering. He is fitted for his role *through* his background. As we have seen, he is an extremely shrewd negotiator, and—as we will see—a great fighter. Had he been raised in comfort and ease, he never would have become anyone like this. His life has prepared and qualified him to bring salvation. In this, he again presents us with a pale shadow of the greater Savior. Jesus "came to that which was his own, but his own did not receive him" (John 1:11). He spent time in the wilderness and was "tempted in every way … yet was without sin" (Hebrews 4:15). And his rejected, yet (unlike Jephthah's) wholly righteous, life prepared him for his ultimate act of weakness, a criminal's death, and qualified him for his greatest victory—to bear sin through that death so that he could give his people his righteousness and lead them into peace.

Questions for reflection

1. Have you experienced the temptation to worship an idol more because it has not delivered? Where did it lead you?

2. Do you want God, or what God gives you? Which aspects of God's perfection will you meditate on so that you love him more than you love his blessings?

3. How would you use the Gileadites' treatment of God and of Jephthah to answer someone who says: *I am a follower of God, and I see Jesus as a great prophet / guide / philosopher?*

PART TWO

The Pen Before the Sword

Jephthah does not go to war immediately. First, he seeks a peaceful resolution: "What do you have against us that you have attacked our country?" (Judges **11:12**). The king of Ammon justifies his attack by claiming that part of the land Israel now lives in formerly belonged to the Ammonites (**v 13**).

In response, Jephthah uses three arguments to refute this claim:

- *Historical (v 15-22)*. Jephthah sets the record straight. When Israel came from Egypt, the Edomites and Moabites lived in the land south of the Arnon. Israel asked both for permission to pass through their land, but were refused (**v 16-18**). Then they traveled towards the land in question, north of the Arnon and south of the Jabbok rivers, where the Amorites under King Sihon lived (**v 19**). Sihon attacked them (**v 20**). Israel won the battle and so won the land by right of conquest (**v 21**). The land was never the Ammonites' (who lived north of the Jabbok), and it was won by Israel fairly from the Amorites.

- *Theological (v 23-24)*. Jephthah uses an assumption held in common by all the peoples of that time and place. The Lord, the God of Israel, obviously gave Israel the land of the Amorites, by enabling them to defeat Sihon (**v 23**). Surely, the Ammonites would do the same if their god, Chemosh, gave them a victory (**v 24**). By using their own religious premises, Jephthah argues that the Lord, the God of Israel, gave them the land. There are two ways of reading Jephthah's words here. One (the more positive) is that he is accommodating himself to the Ammonites' worldview—namely, that each nation's god "gives" that nation a portion of the land—even though as an Israelite he knows this is a mistaken view, because the Lord is the only God, and rules all nations. The other (more negative) option is that Jephthah is himself adopting that worldview—that he knows so little of the God of Israel that he does see him as one god among many. I take the first view, though given what follows, it is clear that Jephthah has adopted some pagan ideas about how to relate to God.

- *Legal precedent (v 25-27)*. Jephthah reminds them that the king of Moab at that time did not think it necessary to attack Israel in the land north of the Arnon (**v 25**). He did not challenge Israel's right to the land—and neither did the Ammonites' ancestors (**v 26**). So why should they do so now?

All three arguments prove it is the Ammonites who are in the wrong, not God's people. But "the king of Ammon, however, paid no attention to the message Jephthah sent him" (**v 28**). He neither replies nor retreats. Truth must be told, and peace sought; but it does not always win the day. After all, the Lord Jesus "committed no sin, and no deceit was found in his mouth. When [his accusers] hurled their insults at him, he did not retaliate; when he suffered, he made no threats. Instead [as Jephthah did in Judges **11:27**], he entrusted himself to him who judges justly" (1 Peter 2:22-23). We follow a Savior whose truth was mocked, and whose righteousness was ignored, and yet who compromised on neither. Jephthah partially, and Christ supremely, have left us an example of how to answer unfair accusations (v 21).

A Terrible Vow

With diplomacy exhausted, war is inevitable. "Then the Spirit of the LORD came upon Jephthah" (Judges **11:29**). From this point, the outcome is certain. But as Jephthah advances to meet the enemy (**v 29**), he "made a vow to the LORD"—if God grants him victory (which we already know, and Jephthah *should* already know, he will), then Jephthah will sacrifice to God the first thing to leave his house when he returns in triumph (**v 30-31**).

"Then Jephthah went over to fight"—and the LORD gives him a total victory (**v 32-33**). So he "returned to his home in Mizpah" (**v 34**), a victorious judge of Israel. Now should follow peace. But...

The first thing out of the door is his daughter, his only child (**v 34**). Jephthah is distraught—he half-blames his daughter, and bemoans the reality that "I have made a vow to the LORD that I cannot break" (**v 35**). His daughter, remarkably, insists that her father keep his word (**v 36**), and after two months to mourn the life she will not have (**v 37-38**), "she returned to her father and he did to her as he had vowed" (**v 39**).

> This is perhaps the worst story in a terrible portion of Israel's history.

This is a terrible story—perhaps the worst in what is an increasingly terrible portion of Israel's history. It begs three questions:

Exactly what had Jephthah promised God? Many people have interpreted Jephthah as promising God an animal sacrifice—so he was expecting an animal to come out to meet him when he returned, and was planning to offer up that animal. But there are three reasons why that is not a right reading. First, it is unlikely that such homes had animals inside ("out of the door of my house," **v 31**). Second, if an animal was meant, the noun would have been in a different form—appropriate for a "neuter" object—but it is not. And third, if Jephthah had promised God an animal, then when his daughter came through the doors he would never have considered the promise to have had any binding force with regard to her.

A few other well-meaning interpreters have read his daughter's lament that she would never marry (**v 37-38**) and suggested that all Jephthah vowed was that she would be condemned to perpetual virginity. But the request for a two-month reprieve (**v 37**) before the sentence is carried out makes no sense unless he literally sacrificed her life. In short, Jephthah did promise to make a human sacrifice to God if God gave him victory. He obviously expected it to be a servant or someone else—not his only child. Jephthah promised human sacrifice to God.

Why did Jephthah promise this? Deuteronomy 12:31 says that human sacrifice is "detestable" and something "the LORD hates." There is no doubt about God's will in the matter. Why then does Jephthah make the vow?

First, Jephthah had clearly been deeply de-sensitized to violence by the atrocious cruelty of the pagan cultures around him. This is a most vivid and horrible example of how believers can profess faith in God and hold on to some truth, yet let the world squeeze them into its mold (see Romans 12:2; Ephesians 4:22-24). Because the culture around Jephthah was violent, he let that worldly violence come in and live alongside his other true beliefs. Today, we are more likely to let worldly attitudes toward sex and money come in and live alongside other true beliefs. Paul says: "Do not be conformed to this world, but be transformed by the renewal of your mind" (Romans 12:2, ESV).

Second, Jephthah was not only infected by pagan moral codes, but also by the pagan works-righteousness understanding of God's character. Human sacrifice was how you could "buy off" a pagan god. A pagan worshipper did human sacrifice to say: *Let me show you how impressed and awed I am by your power.* But the God of the Bible wants only one kind of human sacrifice—the self-sacrifice of offering God the lordship of every area of our lives. Even this is not to secure his favor, but in response to it: "In view of God's mercy … offer your bodies as living sacrifices, holy and pleasing to God—this is your spiritual act of worship" (Romans 12:1). Jephthah thought the LORD needed to be 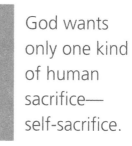 impressed, bought and controlled through a lavish "gift." The tragedy is that God had already decided to save his sinful people (Judges 10:16), and to use Jephthah to do so (**11:29**).

Why did he then keep his vow? This is the hardest one to answer. The best answer is an extension of the same reason that he made it.

God wants only one kind of human sacrifice— self-sacrifice.

Jephthah seems to have no concept of a God of grace. He sees God as basically like the pagan gods—a being whose favor can be earned through flattery and lavish sacrifices. And when he obviously realizes his rash vow has trapped him (**v 35**), why does he not simply confess its sinful foolishness and break it and save his daughter? The answer is: he does not trust God. He is trapped by his mistrust of God. He seems to believe that God will strike him down if he doesn't keep it. This is the same pagan, works-righteousness view of God that led him to make the vow.

The Lessons of Jephthah's Tragedy

Clearly, this episode teaches us to be careful with our words. Once said, they cannot be unsaid. We need to pray, with the psalmist, that God would "set a guard over my mouth" (Psalm 141:3). And it reminds us that God can write straight with crooked pencils. We must beware of mistaking God's work *through* us for evidence that God has finished his work *in* us. Just because we are good speakers, leaders or teachers, and just because God is using us, does not mean our hearts are pleasing to him.

But there are two deeper lessons, as well. First, we are mostly far more affected by our culture than by the Bible—and we are far more affected by our culture than we think. It is easy for us to see how Jephthah ignored what the Scriptures he had (the first five books of our Bible) told him about who God is, and how sacred human life is; how, instead, he listened to pagan culture about God and about life.

> Jephthah makes us ask: *What blindspots do I have?*

But surely many people at other times and places would be astounded at (for example) how much money Christians in western culture spend on themselves. Jephthah makes us look at ourselves and ask: *What enormous blindspots do I have?* If we really want to know the answer to that question, we will be regular and humble Bible-readers.

Second, God's people struggle to believe in a God of grace. In the **Garden of Eden**, the first lie of the serpent was to make humans disbelieve that God had their best interests in mind (Genesis 3:1-5). Since then, we have always felt we have to control God, to pay God and deserve God; that we cannot simply trust God to love and bless us. It is worth asking: *In what ways would I live differently—more radically or restfully—if I really believed God was completely committed to me to love me and bless me and work what is best for me?*

War Within Israel

As in Gideon's time, the men of Ephraim are angry that they have missed out on the glory of victory. This time they go further than complaining, and threaten the judge's life (Judges **12:1**).

In response, Jephthah justifies his position (**v 2-3**), just as he did with the king of the Ammonites (11:15-27). But this time, he does not wait for a response. He "called together the men of Gilead and fought against Ephraim [and] struck them down" because they had been insulted by them (**12:4**). The Ephraimites had held the line of the Jordan against Israel's enemies (3:27-29; 7:24-25); now, Jephthah holds it against them. 42,000 members of the people of God die at the hands of the people of God (**v 6**). Unsurprisingly, the narrator records that Jephthah was judge for six years; but not, unlike all the other judges until now, that he brought peace (**v 7**). Ephraimite blood in the Jordan had ruined that.

Jephthah was careful to be diplomatic and peaceful when his own position was at stake (11:4-11), and when facing the enemies of God's people (v 12-28). But here, he does not hesitate to strike out at those within God's people who oppose him. He treats God's people far worse than he does himself or the world. We are not so different. If we spent as much time pursuing unity and overlooking insults within our churches as we do seeking to remain on good terms with the world, our communities would be far less divided and far more loving. We need to ask: *Where am I too quick to judge my fellow Christians?*

What differences within Christianity do I use as opportunities to look down on others? Who am I refusing to forgive, relishing deep down the opportunity to shun them? Again, we see that all too often, the church's greatest problem is the church!

Questions for reflection

1. Reflect on how you dealt with the last unfair accusation or criticism you faced (from outside or inside the church). How will Jephthah's and Jesus' examples shape your response next time it happens?

2. Meditate on the questions at the bottom of page 120 and top of page 121.

3. Meditate on the questions at the bottom of page 121 and top of page 122.

9. SAMSON: A MIRACULOUS BIRTH

Samson is the last of the God-appointed leaders in Judges. He is famous for the incident which proved both his downfall and paved the way for his greatest act; the cutting of his hair by his wife, Delilah. But his story is much richer than that. In Samson, we see the flaws of God's people between the time of Joshua and the God-given monarchy (and, indeed, every other age between Eden and the New Jerusalem); and yet also in Samson, we see wonderful hints of the perfect Judge and Savior to come. Those hints begin even before he is born.

The Last Minor Judges

12:8-15 records the last of the "non-cyclical" judges. And just as each of the major judges has been further from the ideal of Othniel, achieving a more compromised peace for the people, so these minor judges are a far cry from the ideal minor judge, Shamgar (3:31). Ibzan uses his position to create a familial power base through marriage alliances (**12:9**). After Elon's leadership (**v 10**), Abdon's forty sons and thirty grandsons (**v 14**) indicate he lived like a king, with a harem (as Gideon had done—8:29-31). Seating them on donkeys (the steed of monarchs, see 1 Kings 1:38-39; Zechariah 9:9), reinforces the impression that he is attempting to set up a dynasty. The flaws and failings of the major judges are reflected in these final non-cyclical ones—and none of them are recorded as having "saved Israel."

Whose Eyes Matter?

With the beginning of the final cycle, we are told that, as usual, "the Israelites did evil in the eyes of the LORD," with the familiar result that God gives them over to their enemies, in this case the Philistines (**13:1**).

The phrase "did evil in the eyes of the LORD" has been a repeated refrain in Judges (2:11; 3:7, 12; 4:1; 6:1; 10:6)—this is the last time it appears. Although in fact, there is a phrase which appears twice in the double conclusion to the book, which says the same thing in a different way: "in those days … everyone did what was right in his own eyes" (17:6; 21:25, ESV—the NIV obscures the parallel by translating the end of these sentences "did as he saw fit").

The writer is making the point that many of the things the Israelites did were not evil "in their eyes." In other words, by their perception, most or all of their behavior was perfectly acceptable. They did not go about thinking: *I know this is evil, but I am going to do it anyway.* Yet "in God's eyes," the behavior was wicked.

This teaches us two truths about sin. First, *the definition of sin.* This term "the eyes of the LORD," in contrast with our "own eyes," teaches us that sin does not ultimately consist of violating our conscience or violating our personal standards or violating community standards, but rather consists of violating God's will for us.

This flies in the face of modern thinking, of course. It is continually asserted in innumerable forums and venues that "only you can define what's right and wrong for you." In other words, "my own eyes"—my heart's feelings and my mind's perceptions—are the only way to determine right and wrong.

Common sense contradicts this, even if we didn't have the Bible. If evil is only determined by our own eyes, how could we tell the Nazis that it was wrong to exterminate Jews—they thought they were doing the human race a favor, or even providing justice for past imagined "wrongs." But once we admit that "our own eyes" are not sufficient for defining sin, then whose eyes are? Is evil defined by what is so in experts' eyes? Or in the majority's eyes? These views don't avoid holocausts either. No, the Bible's answer is the right one. Sin is defined as violating our relationship with God, as violating the will of God for us. What God sees as sin is sin, regardless of what we feel or the experts say or the culture agrees on.

Second, these phrases show us *the deception of sin*. They remind us how easily self-deceived we are. The Israelites had psychological and cultural rationalizations and supports for their sin, so they were in a kind of "group denial." In their own "eyes" or perception, there was nothing wrong with what they were doing. There was a deep, suppressed knowledge that they were out of touch with God, rejecting his will (Romans 1:18); but at the conscious level, they had no overt guilt and they had lots of explanations for their lifestyles.

We don't know what those rationales were, but we must remember that the heart of their sin (and ours) is idolatry, and idols are not always bad things, but good things turned into ultimate hopes and goals. So the line between hard work and making an idol of work, or loving your family and making an idol of it, is a thin one. And an idol is by its nature deceitful. It tells us we are being sensible, careful and wise to work so hard—even that we are being unselfish—when in fact we have set it in God's place in our hearts, and are thus doing evil in the only eyes in the universe that really count.

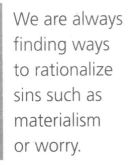
We are always finding ways to rationalize sins such as materialism or worry.

This should lead us to be very careful constantly to evaluate ourselves, through reflection on the Bible and through personal accountability to others. We are always finding ways to rationalize sins such as materialism or worry or bitterness or pride. They don't look bad in "our eyes." As the seventeenth-century Puritan writer, Thomas Brooks, put it: "Satan paints sin with virtue's colors."

You Will Have a Son

In Judges **13:2-3**, we are introduced to Manoah, a Danite, and his wife (who remains nameless, yet is the real heroine of this chapter). And "the angel of the LORD appeared to her" (**v 3**)—God has begun to act to save his people. Samson is the only judge chosen before he is born, or even conceived. Manoah's wife is "sterile and remained childless" (**v 2**). "But," says the angel of LORD, "you are going to conceive and have a son" (**v 3**). She must not drink alcohol, or eat anything unclean (**v 4**), or cut his hair, because this son "is to be a Nazirite, set apart to God from birth, and he will begin the deliverance of Israel from the hands of the Philistines" (**v 5**).

The Nazirite vow to which the angel refers is found in Numbers 6:1-21, and contained three basic stipulations. A Nazirite was not to cut hair during the period of the vow; was not to drink any produce from vines, alcoholic or non-alcoholic; and was not to have contact with any dead body.

The purpose of the Nazirite vow was to ask for God's special help during a crucial time. It was a sign that you were looking to God with great intensity and focus. Keeping one's hair uncut and refraining from the fruit of the vine were ways of showing that you were "in training" toward a goal. By refraining from touching a dead body, you were adopting the stringent rules of ceremonial cleanliness for priests, who were not allowed to touch anything dead because they worked in God's house (the tabernacle, at this point in history) every day. So the Nazirite was living before the presence of God every day.

As is clear from Numbers 6, the Nazirite vow was made voluntarily and for a definite period of time. But Samson was being born into the Nazirite state involuntarily (his parents were taking the vows for him), and he was to stay a Nazirite all his life. His mother was not to drink wine or eat unclean foods, because the Nazirite vow started immediately—when Samson was in her womb! What she ate and drank, Samson-in-utero also would eat and drink. God put Samson under this "rule" even when he was still unborn. He was truly to be "set apart to God from [and before] birth" (Judges **13:5**).

The God of the Impossible

This special birth points us forward, of course, to the most special of all births, over a millennium later. But Jesus' conception is not the only one Samson's should remind us of. God has often worked in the world through a child whose existence, humanly speaking, is impossible.

> God has often worked through a child whose existence is impossible.

Isaac, the son whom God had promised to Abram, and through whom would come blessing to the world (Genesis 12:1-3), was born to Sarah—to a woman who was barren (11:30; 21:1-3). Samuel, whom God would use to anoint the first two chosen kings for his people, was born to a woman who had been unable to bear children, Hannah (1 Samuel 1:5-7, 19-20). John the Baptist, who would announce the coming of the Lord himself, was born to Elizabeth, who was "barren; and ... well along in years" (Luke 1:7). Mary's pregnancy was impossible for a different reason; she was a virgin (Luke 1:26-27, 34). In the birth of Jesus the degree of miraculousness goes off the scale—for all the other babies, God's power opened women's wombs so that they could conceive naturally, but with Mary, God enabled her to conceive without a human father at all.

And apart from Hannah's case, God used an angel to promise the pregnancy. Each birth was something the mother was humanly incapable of—God was showing that the outworking of his salvation promises was something no human could manage; that he alone is the one who "gives life to the dead and calls things that are not as though they were" (Romans 4:17).

There are two important ways in which the birth of Samson, and those of Isaac, Samuel and John, are different from that of Jesus. First, the other births each happened in the shadow of disgrace. In ancient times, a woman's fertility was a major part of her honor and dignity. And Israelite women, remembering God's promise to Eve that a savior would be born who would defeat the devil and undo the effects of sin, would have longed to participate—potentially—in the fulfillment of that promise.

So a woman who could not bear children lived under a cloud of shame, and with a sense of disappointment (at least one of which is still keenly felt by many childless women in our cultures today). God visited in mercy and lifted the shame and disgrace, bringing honor and joy.

But the birth of Jesus *brought* disgrace to mother and son. We should never forget that our Savior was born in scandal and suspicion. This reminds us that while the other "saviors" gained honor and glory in order to do their work, Jesus lost all his honor and glory to do his.

> We should never forget that our Savior was born in scandal and suspicion.

Second, the salvation Samson would bring would be incomplete. He would only "begin the deliverance of Israel from the … Philistines" (Judges **13:5**). Samson is the last judge, but he points beyond himself—beyond the book of Judges—to the one who would complete the victory over the Philistines: to King David, God's king anointed by Samuel (1 Samuel 16:1-13). And David's salvation was also incomplete, because he provided rest from enemies but could not bring victory over the sin of his own heart, far less his people's. Only Jesus' salvation is a complete salvation—in this sense, only he finished the job. As an angel told Mary's fiancé, Joseph: "he will save his people from their sins" (Matthew 1:21). Samson points us to David, and beyond him to the greater David—Jesus.

Questions for reflection

1. How will your life this week reflect the truth that God's eyes matter more than yours?

2. What three things, other than God, do you spend most time thinking about; become most excited about; care most about? How could these things become idols to you? How can you spot it happening?

3. God "gives life to the dead and calls things that are not as though they were" (Romans 4:17). In which part of your life, or at which time of your day, do you most need to enjoy this truth?

PART TWO

Faith and Obedience

When Sarah heard she would become pregnant despite her barrenness, she laughed with disbelief (Genesis 18:9-15). When an angel told John the Baptist's father he would have a son, he could not believe it (Luke 1:13-20). Samson's mother, though, showed complete faith in the LORD's ability to do the impossible—"the woman went to her husband and told him, 'A man of God came to me. He looked like an angel of God, very awesome ... he said to me, "You will conceive and give birth to a son"'" (Judges **13:6-7**). She believed the word from God, delivered through his messenger, just as another woman would 1,200 years later: "May it be to me as you have said" (Luke 1:38).

Further, Samson's mother obeyed the word from God. She accepted the need to apply to herself the Nazirite behavioral code (Judges **13:7**) in order to have a son who was used in God's service; just as another woman would put herself entirely at God's disposal 1,200 years later: "I am the Lord's servant" (Luke 1:38). Both Manoah's wife and Mary trust that God will do what he has planned and promised and, at cost to themselves (Nazirite adherence for Samson's mother, shame and disgrace for Jesus'), become obedient to that plan. This is faith.

Something Better than Rules

Samson's father also shows faith. He asks God to grant them a return visit from "the man ... you sent" (Judges **13:8**). Why? To teach them "how to bring up the boy who is to be born." Some consider this request to be a lack of faith in God—but Manoah assumes that the promise will come true—that a boy will be born. His request is not for proof that they will have a son, but for help to know how to raise the son.

The LORD graciously sends the angel back (**v 9**). Again, he appears to the wife; this time, she fetches her husband (**v 10-11**), so that he can repeat his request for more specific information on how God wants this child to be reared (**v 12**).

But the angel will not give them any more specifics. Their son will be set apart, and Manoah's wife "must do all that I have told her" (**v 13**); but he will give them no more rules.

Manoah—not realizing that this is a heavenly angel rather than a human prophet (**v 16**)—offers food to this messenger (**v 15**). There may be some element of pagan religion here, since in that culture feeding someone (a god, or a person) meant they were obligated to you. Likewise, to know someone's name (**v 17**) was to know their character; it established a relationship, with duties on both sides. Manoah is still trying to get the angel to tell him the rules by which he should bring up his son!

This would explain why the angel will not eat with him (**v 16**—elsewhere, angels do eat with men, eg: Genesis 18:1-8); and why he replies to the question about his name with a question of his own (Judges **13:18**). He is not in Manoah's debt, and will not give him the information he thinks he needs.

Yet why would the angel of the LORD have returned if he had no new information to give? Manoah prayed for help, and that help was apparently refused. But in fact, Manoah *did* get the help he needed, but not in the *form* he was asking for. He wanted to know "what is to be the *rule* for the boy's life and work?" (**v 12**)—to have more regulations. Instead, God gives Manoah a revelation of who he is. As we have seen, the angel of the LORD is likely the Son of God (see pages 74-75). And his name, he says, "is beyond understanding" (**v 18**)—it is too wonderful for a human to grasp. This points Manoah to his glory. Then "the LORD" himself "did an amazing thing ... as the flame blazed up from the altar toward heaven, the angel of the LORD ascended in the flame" (**v 19-20**). He indelibly prints in their minds his greatness.

At last, Manoah "realized that it was the angel of the LORD. 'We are doomed to die!' he said to his wife. 'We have seen God!'"

(**v 21-22**). He knows enough of his people's history to understand that no one can see God's face and live (Exodus 33:20). But while he panics, his wife remains calm. "If the LORD had meant to kill us, he would not have accepted" their sacrifices; nor would he have "shown us all these things" (Judges **13:23**). Evidently, they have *not* died! Interestingly, this reminds us that faith is not the absence of thinking, but it is thinking and acting on the basis of the word and promises of God.

God has not come near to them to destroy them, sinful humans though they are. In this, he shows them his goodness.

So, in reply to being asked about how to bring up their God-given son as part of the outworking of God's plan—how to live his way and please him—the LORD says: *You need to know me and my character far more than you need more information. All the rules in the world would not be able to give you direction in the innumerable decisions and choices you will have to make with your son. Only a deep understanding of who I am can give you the guidance you need.*

As we will see, Samson's own life story—as well as Manoah's attempts to manipulate the angel—indicates that his parents fell quite short in their child-rearing, and failed to show and explain God's character to their son. Yet God's message to them is a message to all of us. We think we need rules, but we need to know God. God does not, and will not, give us a guidebook for every twist and turn, every doubt and decision in our lives. He gives us something much better—he gives us himself.

> God gives us something much better than a guidebook—he gives us himself.

Conformed or Transformed?

It is worth pausing on this point a little longer. In general, a parent gives a child fewer details as he or she gets older. When your child is very little, you must virtually follow them around and say: *Don't touch this* and *Don't go here* every step of the way! A child doesn't know not to put his finger in a wall socket, and doesn't know not to eat dirt. They need to conform to your commands.

The older a child gets, the more you expect them to incorporate the parent's values and thinking and wisdom into their own heart so that they don't need detailed instructions all the time. In order to guide children into maturity, parents must increasingly move from lots of external rules to internal motives and principles of wisdom.

In the same way, Christians in the New Testament receive far fewer rules and regulations than believers in the Old Testament. In the Old Testament, so much of what you could wear and eat and do was prescribed. And then on the priest's ephod, there were the Urim and Thummim, which gave *yes* and *no* answers to direct questions to God! What a huge amount of guidance and therefore certainty they could have! Many Christians consider this a more advanced level of guidance than we have today. Like Manoah, we would like to have considerably more regulations.

But that is to mistake external rules for a mature relationship. Paul says that the Christian is not to be "conformed," but rather, "transformed by the renewing of your mind" (Romans 12:2). We don't get lots of prescriptions; we do, through the Holy Spirit, get God, and enjoy knowing "the mind of Christ" (1 Corinthians 2:16). We can look at his rescue on the cross, and his resurrection in triumph, and see the character of God much more clearly than even the greatest heroes in the Old Testament could. We don't need to know about God through his external standards when we can know God through his Spirit. We need to remember the lesson Manoah was taught!

What's in a Name?

All this has happened before Samson is even born! But his birth is not in doubt, since it rests on God's promise. And so "the woman gave birth to a boy and named him Samson" (Judges **13:24**), a name which means "little sun." Since the sun was considered a god by many

Canaanites, this is another clue that Israel, while not rejecting the LORD outright, have combined half-hearted worship of him with worship of other nations' deities. It is concerning that a future judge of Israel —a forerunner of God's Son—is himself named after a pagan god, being effectively called "Sun-son."

Nevertheless, God is at work for and through his flawed people. As Samson grows up, he is blessed by God (**v 24**), and God's Spirit begins to work in him (**v 25**). This is a boy conceived miraculously, chosen by God, set apart to serve him, blessed by him and shaped by his Spirit. Samson has every spiritual advantage. He is the last judge in this book, the last great hope for Israel. We wait to see how he will rescue and rule God's people in obedience to God.

And in almost every way, we will find ourselves disappointed. Samson's flaws, just as much as his birth, will remind us that God's people need another, greater Deliverer.

Questions for reflection

1. What difference does it make to our obedience when we act out of faith in God's promises, rather than a grudging duty to obey?

2. In what parts of your life would you, deep down, like God to give you rules or answers, instead of himself?

3. Are there ways in which you are not enjoying your relationship with the living God, because you would rather have some regulations to follow?

10. SAMSON: THE WOMANIZER

The story of Samson is famous for its potent mix of sex, violence, death and power—exactly the stuff of a contemporary summer action film! But if we read it as part of the whole narrative of the book of Judges, we will find it to be at least perplexing and probably disturbing. As Israel's spiritual condition grows worse and worse, the scene seems to be set for a great judge/leader, perhaps the greatest of all. And chapter 13, with its **annunciation**, prepares us for a wonderful, powerful deliverer.

Instead, we find by far the most flawed character in the book: a violent, impulsive, sexually addicted, emotionally immature and selfish man. Most disturbing of all, the "Spirit of God" seems to anoint and use his fits of pique, pride, and temper.

A Philistine Woman

Samson is now a grown man, stirred by the Spirit of the Lord (13:25). But at the start of chapter 14—and throughout the rest of his life—he will be stirred by a much more worldly impulse. One day, he "went down to Timnah and saw there a young Philistine woman" (**14:1**). Returning home, he says (literally) to his parents: "have *I* seen a woman, in Timnah, of the daughters of the Philistines. Now get her for me as a wife" (**v 2**).

His parents no doubt remember the angel's prediction that Samson would deliver the Israelites from the Philistines (it's not the kind of thing you would forget!). So imagine their distress when Samson comes home and, instead of fighting Israel's enemies, wants to marry one of them! They protest that there must be a woman in their wider family, or at least in Israel, whom he could marry (**v 3**): "Must you go to the uncircumcised Philistines to get a wife?" The word "uncircumcised" is key here. Circumcision was a sign that a family was in a personal covenant or relationship with God, as part of his people. Their issue was not a racial one (*No son of mine will marry one of those Philistines!*). It is about marriage with someone outside of the LORD's covenant. God's prohibition (Exodus 34:15-16) is not against inter-racial marriage, but against inter-faith marriage (for instance, Moses was married to a non-Israelite, Zipporah, but one who recognized God's covenant; see Exodus 4:24-26).

But Samson is not willing to listen. "Get her for me," he rudely insists (Judges **14:3**). He then says (literally): "She is right in my eyes." This is the approach to life and morality that we have seen all Israel adopting: doing what was evil in God's eyes, because it was right in their own (13:1; 17:6). Samson is a leader who reflects Israel's real spiritual state, rather than God's ideal for his people. Here we are seeing Israel writ small, in one man's life. (In chapters 17 – 21, we will see the same impulses and spiritual rottenness writ far larger, and still more horrifically.)

> In Samson we are seeing Israel writ small, in one man's life.

First, Samson is impulsive. He is a completely sensual man, in the most basic definition of the term. His senses control him—he reacts to how he feels about what he sees, without reflection or consideration. He sees—and so he takes. This general impulsiveness leads to a specific weakness that we will see as the story proceeds; namely, a total lack of sexual self-control.

Second, Samson is unteachable. He is dismissive of parental counsel and authority. The book of Proverbs extensively explains how proud and foolish it is to be unwilling to listen to the advice of others. Put in its cultural context, Samson's pride here is even more extreme. In our day it would be more normal for a son to talk back to his parents, but that was not the case in ancient Israel. Arthur E. Cundall says:

> "In Israelite society the father was the head of the family and as such exercised control … including the choice of wives for sons (eg: Genesis 24:4; 38:6). It was exceptional for a son to contravene the wishes of his parents in this … realm (Genesis 26:34-35), for the unit was the clan and personal preference was subordinated to it."   (*Judges and Ruth*, page 162)

Impulsive, and unteachable. It is a good summary of the state of Israel as a whole!

Unequal Yokes

We need to take a brief diversion here, to think about *why* the Bible commands believers not to enter unequal marriages. Exodus 34:15-16 tells Israel neither to make a treaty with "those who live in the land" (ie: those who don't know the LORD), nor to "choose some of their daughters as wives for your sons." Why? Because such binding partnerships, whether at a national or familial level, will cause Israel to join their allies/wives as they "prostitute themselves to their gods" (v 16).

In 2 Corinthians 6:14-16, the apostle Paul renews the appeal to believers to not enter into binding partnerships with those who do not worship God. (The word "yoked" probably means several kinds of binding relationships, but it must at the very least mean marriage, which is the most binding of all human relationships.) Here, as in Exodus, the main issue is that such marriages weaken a believer's loyalty to God—"what agreement is there between the temple of God and idols?" (v 16).

A superficial reading of Paul's statement might lead a reader to conclude that the Bible is concerned that the unbelieving spouse will try to convert the believer. So sometimes people say: *This is no problem for me. I can marry X because he or she completely respects my faith and will allow me total freedom to practice it.* But remember, the context for each of these texts is not other formal religions, but idolatry. Idolatry is displacing God by making good, created things more important than God. When your spouse doesn't share your faith, there is great pressure to adapt to that by pushing God more to the margins of your life. You are in an intimate relationship with someone who does not understand what should be the very mainspring of, and motivation for, absolutely everything you do. The natural response to this is to make God less central to everything. Otherwise you will constantly be getting blank stares from your mate. There is a daily, unseen pressure to worship something else: your spouse him/herself, or the idols that they bring to the marriage (probably without realizing it).

This is the reason the Bible urges believers to not knowingly marry an unbeliever. (We should remember, however, that Paul insists that a Christian who is already married to a non-Christian should not seek divorce from him or her but should actively seek to build a good marriage—1 Corinthians 7:12-15.)

What Israel Didn't Do

We can already see that Samson is not going to be the judge we were hoping for! The first judge, Othniel, fought Israel's enemies and so married Acsah, a godly, faithful, trusting Israelite (Judges 1:12-13). The last, Samson, goes among Israel's enemies in order to marry an unnamed Philistine who does not know God. It is important that he found her in Timnah—deep in Israelite territory—and that he was free to come and go among the Philistines. The Philistines were settled and living normal lives inside Israel. They were "rulers" (13:1; **14:4**) over Israel, yet their "occupation" seems completely peaceful. Samson thought nothing of marrying one of them.

This should prompt us to realize that something has been missing from this Judges cycle. *Israel has not cried out for rescue from oppression.* There is no resistance to their enslavement. Later in the narrative, the men of Judah (who had been the first to go up to fight for their land, 1:2), simply take it as a fact of life that "the Philistines are rulers over us" (15:11).

In short, Israel's capitulation to the Philistines is far more profound and complete than any of their previous enslavements. In the past, Israel groaned and agonized under their occupations by pagan powers, because their domination was military and political. But now the people are virtually unconscious of their enslavement, because its nature is that of cultural accommodation. The Israelites do not groan and resist their "captors" now because they have completely adopted and adapted to the values, **mores** and idols of the Philistines. Like Samson himself, the Israelites were eager to marry into Philistine society, probably as a way to "move up" in the culture. The Israelites no longer had a recognizable culture of their own, one based on service to the LORD.

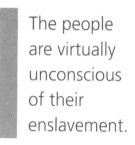

The people are virtually unconscious of their enslavement.

We can't exaggerate the danger to Israel. The Israelites were on the brink of extinction. Within a couple of generations, they could have been completely **assimilated** into the Philistine nation. Michael Wilcock says:

> "There is no such thing as harmonious co-existence between the church and the world, for where there is no conflict it is because the world has taken over."
>
> (*The Message of Judges*, page 142)

Here are three examples of how the church's efforts at avoiding conflict with the world have been, or are now, really a surrender to the world:

- In the first half of the 20th century, mainline Protestants made a very bold move to be "relevant" to modern people who could not believe in the supernatural. Rudolph Bultmann, a major theologian, said: "No one who uses modern technology can believe in the ancient world of spirits and miracles." It was thought that modern people would eventually completely lose all belief in a supernatural world. So many churches began the project of "de-supernaturalizing" the Christian message. The Bible was no longer seen as an **infallible** revelation from God, but as inspiring—though flawed—ancient stories. The very concepts of "conversion" and "the new birth" were dropped. Now, to "become a Christian" meant to live a good life of mercy and justice. This took away the "conflict" between Christianity and those who could not believe in miracles, a divinely revealed Bible, or a physical resurrection. But of course, this meant that scientific rationalism was now the real "ruler."

■ Those churches which we can, for the sake of convenience, call "liberal," appeal to a section of modern culture which has (at least) three idols: (1) personal choice and freedom; (2) absolute tolerance and the rejection of exclusive truth and personal responsibility; (3) professional expertise and status. Such churches, in order to attract this culture and avoid conflict, have adapted. They accept modern sex ethics, they do not do church discipline, they do not preach Christ as the only way to salvation. Their ministry is supportive and therapeutic, and no one is ever warned of the dangers of God's judgment. The church is run by experts and the laity are not empowered to minister. In general, the popular opinions of modern culture are adopted and promoted. If churches preached judgment, accountability and moral virtue (as Jesus did)—there would be conflict!

■ More "conservative" churches appeal to those who idolize: (1) an idealized past; (2) the nuclear family; (3) one's own race and traditional culture; (4) authority. While liberal culture is relativistic, conservative culture is moralistic and makes an idol out of "goodness" and respectability. Conservative culture often values unquestioning deference to leaders, tends to idealize "the good old days," tends to feel superior in its view of its own culture, and tends to put so much emphasis on family life that singles and single parents feel like second-class citizens. If churches preached about racism, the need for justice for the poor, and challenged people to embrace the socially and morally unrespectable (as Jesus did)—there would be conflict!

In Samson's Israel, God had decided to prevent his people becoming culturally indistinct, and therefore spiritually extinct. He would do so through Samson, and despite Samson. And there would be conflict!

Questions for reflection

1. When do you find it hardest not to act on impulse?

2. Do you need to wrestle with the implications of 2 Corinthians 6 for your own life, or speak to a Christian friend about this issue?

3. Why is assimilation into the surrounding culture so attractive for churches, and for individual believers? How do you feel that pressure in your own life?

PART TWO

Working Through Sin

What does God do when his people are not just accommodating, but becoming assimilated into, the world? **14:4** is the crucial verse in the Samson narrative, the key to understanding the whole story, and the answer to that question. "His parents did not know that this [Samson's overriding desire to marry the Philistine] was from the LORD, who was seeking an occasion to confront the Philistines."

God will use the very weaknesses of Samson—his "fraternization" with the Philistines, his sexual appetite, his vindictiveness and temper (both of which we will see in the next part)—to bring about confrontation between the two nations. Samson's weaknesses result in a "blood feud" that leads to more and more conflict, and finally the division between the two nations that is so desperately needed.

Michael Wilcock puts it well:

"The force of 14:4 is that the two communities are so interlocked that even the Lord can find nothing to get hold of to pry them apart. He uses Samson's weaknesses, therefore, to bring about the relationship with this irresistible girl from which so much ill-feeling will flow." (*The Message of Judges,* page 139)

As the story goes on, we will see everyone acting out of their own ungodly character. They are all responsible for what they do. But we will also see God using it all to ensure that the two nations are alienated (despite Samson's, and then Judah's, best efforts), so that his people will not totally lose their distinctiveness. God remains unconditionally committed to his covenant promises. He has promised to love them and give them an inheritance and never break his commitment to do so (2:1). Here, he is so faithful to his promises that he not only fulfills them *in spite of* their

God fulfills his promises not only *in spite of* sin, but even *through* sin.

sin, but even *through* their sin. He uses their own sinfulness to bring about deliverance.

The supreme example of this is in Acts 2:23, where we see that God used the free, wicked choices of human beings to put Jesus to death, therefore redeeming the world from free, wicked choices! Though the people who put Jesus to death were doing so wickedly, God arranged things so their wickedness only fulfilled redemptive purposes.

So, strange though it seems, God in his mercy is using his people's weaknesses to make sure there is not peace between them and the surrounding cultures. God's people (today as then) need to not be at peace with the world—because "friendship with the world is hatred toward God" (James 4:4). Why? Because if we are like the world, we will love idols and forsake God; we will, as James puts it, be "adulterous people." It is the mercy of God that he does not allow the world to love the church for very long. It forces his people to recognize that we are not part of the world—that we have a different Lord and Savior—and finally cry out to him to rescue us from ourselves and rule us despite ourselves.

A Lion, a Bet, and a Woman

We have taken most of this chapter to cover four verses—now we cover the rest of chapters 14 and 15 in a few pages! But these two chapters are in essence the outworking of who Samson is (impulsive, and unteachable); who Israel are (virtually indistinguishable from the nations around them); and what God is doing (rescuing his people by prompting conflict with their physical and spiritual masters).

The first and third of these themes are in focus in **14:5 – 15:8**. Samson begins to show disdain for his Nazirite vow. When "a young lion came roaring towards him … he tore the lion apart with his bare hands" (**14 v 5-6**). As a Nazirite, he cannot touch a dead animal, and should now go straight to the tabernacle for cleansing. But he is on his way to see the woman he wants—clearly his lust overwhelms his vows, so he does not tell his parents (**v 6**) and he "went down and talked with the woman" (**v 7**). Later, he again touches a dead animal, and this time causes his parents unwittingly to become unclean too (**v 8-9**).

Samson prepares to marry his bride (**v 10-11**), and, in effect, gambles with his Philistine "companions" (**v 12-14**), betting that they will not crack his riddle and he will gain wealth. But the Philistines lean on his wife (who at this stage is pledged to him, though the wedding itself has not yet happened), and, displaying once again his inability to think rationally when confronted with a woman he likes the look of, Samson tells her the answer, and she passes it on (**v 15-18**). Now we see the vindictive violence of Samson (**v 19**). As we've seen, he cannot control his senses, and he cannot control his temper. He strikes down thirty Philistines, not from a desire to save Israel, but to get even and to pay his debts.

> Samson cannot control his senses or his temper.

Because Samson returns to his parents' house, his wife is "given to the friend who had attended him" (**v 20**)—ie: a Philistine. But Samson cannot know this, so "later on … [he] went to visit his wife" (**15:1**). We might expect him, feelings-driven as he is, to accept the new offer of the younger, prettier sister (**v 2**), but no one tells Samson what to do! "This time I have a right to get even with the Philistines; I will really harm them" (**v 3**)—and the result of his violent anger this time is to burn the Philistine fields (**v 4-5**). In retaliation for Samson's retaliation, the Philistines "burned her [Samson's wife] and her father to death" (**v 6**). Samson, as we would expect, won't take this lightly—he swears revenge (**v 7**) and "slaughtered many of them" (**v 8**).

No one comes out of this episode well. Samson does not care at all about his God-given role, and is brutally violent; but the Philistines, one of whom offers such a thug two of his daughters, and who is then burned to death by his countrymen, are just as bad. Samson is just like God's enemies. As we've already said, it's easy for us to look at another culture and see how a member of God's people has "sold out" to the surrounding culture; we're far more unwilling to look hard at where we might have done so.

The Spirit of the Lord

But in all this, God is at work. Why can Samson kill the lion? "The Spirit of the Lord came upon him in power" (**14:6**). Why is he able to strike down thirty Philistines to steal their clothes? "The Spirit of the Lord came upon him in power" (**v 19**). God is giving Samson super-human strength—the one thing he needs (other than his own character flaws) for him to cause the division between Israel and the Philistines which God's people, though they don't realize it, desperately need. God is starting to save his people by divorcing them from their marriage to their idols and to the world around them.

But how can God use such flawed people—people like Samson—to get his work done? Shouldn't he only work with people who are good, godly men and women? Shouldn't he only use the people who have the right beliefs, and the right behavior?

> God saves his people by divorcing them from their marriage to their idols.

The problem with this is that it puts God in a box. It would mean he is limited by humans, and is only allowed to work when people are being good and making godly choices. It would mean that God does not work by grace, taking the initiative to save; but that he works in response to good works, waiting for people to help him to save.

David Jackman describes how Judges "shoots holes through all of that:"

"It is above all a book about grace, undeserved mercy, as is the whole Bible ... That is not to play down theological accuracy or to pretend it doesn't matter how we behave ... [We will still suffer from our sins]. But we can rejoice that he is also in the business of using our failures as the foundations for his success. Let us never imagine that we have God taped, or that we know how he will work, or when. As soon as we start to say, 'God cannot or will not… until…' we are wrong-footed."

(*Judges, Ruth*, page 222)

The amazing truth is that God works through sinners, and through sinful situations. He keeps his promises to bless his people in the dark and disastrous periods of our lives, as well as through the times when things are going "right." Not even our own sin will stop him saving us, or using us. Mysteriously, often unseen, and usually far beyond our comprehension, God works through the free (and very often flawed) choices people make: "In *all* things, God works for the good of those who love him" (Romans 8:28).

Leadership Without Peace

The violence is ratcheting up, retaliation after retaliation. Without forgiveness and reconciliation, it is a familiar story to us, both within family structures and on national levels. Each action prompts a reaction, which brings its own reaction, and the seemingly unbreakable cycle continues. And so the Philistines take up arms and make camp in Judah, "to take Samson prisoner … to do to him as he did to us" (**15:10**). Judah is so keen to remain at peace with them that they have no idea that God has raised up a judge to save Israel (**v 10**)! And when they discover that he has, they send 3,000 men to hand the judge over to their enemy (**v 11-12**)! They may bear the name of God's people, but they would rather live at peace with the world and worship their idols than be freed to worship God—and they would rather cut down their own rescuer than risk confrontation with the world.

So they tie up their own judge (**v 13**), and take him to the Philistines. Again, though, "the Spirit of the Lord came upon him in power." Samson breaks his bonds, and "finding a fresh jawbone of a donkey"—a dead animal, though Samson seems to have left his Nazirite vow well behind by now—"he grabbed it and struck down a thousand men" (**v 14-15**), taunting them as he kills them (**v 16**).

Now, for the first time, Samson speaks to the God who has chosen him, and empowered him. But his prayer is neither humble nor faithful: he basically demands that God help him, and complains that he doesn't (**v 18**)—which is remarkably clueless of him, since it is God's Spirit which has rescued him from a lion, from a lost bet, and now from a thousand Philistines. Samson uses God's strength, but he doesn't depend on God except when he is in extreme situations (he won't speak to him again until 16:28, when he is blind and trapped). Yet God is at work through Samson, and provides the water he needs (**15:19**). Thus refreshed, "Samson led Israel for twenty years" (**v 20**). But it is not the leadership of the earlier judges. He has not saved Israel from spiritual or physical oppression—it is still "the days of the Philistines."

Gift-giving and Fruit-growing

Again, Samson is gifted by the Spirit in a remarkable way—killing a thousand armed men with a jaw bone is no mean feat! But if Samson has God's Spirit, shouldn't we see him growing in holiness? How can he be so empowered by the Spirit, and yet show no patience, humility or self-control?

But the Bible has always made a distinction that most believers are unaware of. It is possible to have the gifts of the Spirit, yet lack the fruit of the Spirit. In 1 Corinthians 12 and 14, Paul tells us that "gifts" of the Spirit are skills for *doing*—abilities for serving and helping people, though they can be used for other ends, too. But in Galatians 5:22-23, Paul tells us that the "fruit" of the Spirit is character traits of *being*—qualities such as peace, patience, gentleness, self-control. Then in 1 Corinthians 13:1-3, Paul tells us that it is possible to have skills (or gifts) of teaching and speaking and leadership—and yet lack the fruit of love, without which gifts are worth "nothing."

So we will at times in Scripture come across men and women—like Samson—who have great gifts, but seem very shallow in holiness and character. And 1 Corinthians 13 means that we should beware this in ourselves, too. The gifts of the Holy Spirit can operate in us, even mightily, and we can be helping people and leading movements—yet our inner personal lives can still be a complete wreck. In fact, this pattern is so common that there may regularly be a link between an impressive outer life and a broken inner life. Some people who are the most vigorous and effective in teaching, counseling, and leadership are, in their private lives, giving in to temptation, discouragement, anger, and fear.

What can we do about it? First, we can recognize the biblical distinction between gifts and fruit. Many people look at their gifts as a self-justifying "proof" that they are fine spiritually: *Look at the people I serve and who tell me how much I mean to them! Surely God is pleased with me.* But we must not mistake the operation of gifts for the growth of fruit. The fruit is the "proof" of spiritual growth.

Second, our prayer life, rather than our religious activities, is the best indicator of spiritual health. Is prayer warm, enjoyable, consistent? Are you not only talking but listening and learning? Or, like Samson, do you only pray as a last resort, and only for yourself and your own desires?

> Our prayer life is the best indicator of our spiritual health.

Third, we must avoid "Lone Ranger" Christianity. Intimate fellowship is the best way to ensure the integrity of our inner and outer lives. Samson is notable for his aloneness. Not only does he not take any advice, but he never works with others, or builds teams. He is a one-man wrecking crew. That is a prescription for focusing on outward impressiveness while suffering from internal disintegration, since no one is close enough to see our spiritual lives, or to encourage and challenge us about it.

Questions for reflection

1. How have you seen the Lord working through your sin, or someone else's sin? How does this lead you to praise him?

2. Why is it exciting and liberating, as well as humbling, to know that God works through flawed people?

3. What do your prayers reveal about your view of gifts of the Spirit and the fruit of the Spirit? Are you being prompted to pray more, or differently?

11. SAMSON: THE WEAK VICTOR

Samson, the judge and appointed savior of God's people, has now killed over a thousand Philistines, without in any way leading Israel toward freedom and obedience to the Lord. All his actions against the Philistines have been self-serving, to get him out of the trouble that followed his decision to go to the Philistine town of Timnah, where he "saw … a young Philistine woman" (14:1).

But by the end of chapter 15, Samson has escaped the Philistines' clutches, and leads Israel for twenty years. And then, "one day Samson went to Gaza"—not just a Philistine town, but their capital—"where he saw a prostitute" (**16:1**). Samson has learned nothing! And, while his physical strength will once again rescue him from his own weakness for women, the next difficulty he gets into will be his last.

The Pattern Continues

Verses 1-3 are thus a link both to the past (14:1 – 15:20) and to the future (**16:4-31**). They're typical of the pattern of Samson's life—being enticed into an extremely dangerous situation because of his weakness for women. For Israel's judge to spend the night with a *Philistine* prostitute (**v 1**), allowing himself to be surrounded (**v 2**), is not just disobedient, it is foolish.

It also shows how that pattern is deepening—his recklessness (in going to the capital), his sexual addiction (sleeping with a prostitute) and the strength of the trap (surrounded by guards in a walled city, **v 2-3**), are all greater than they were in the previous two chapters.

Like any pattern of addiction or compulsion, the cycle is increasing in force and power. And the act of strength required to break out is the most impressive yet—it is a remarkable feat to lift a city gate, and carry it forty miles to a hill near Hebron, as Samson does in **verse 3**.

We know by now that Samson does not learn. We will expect increasing recklessness and danger, and an outstanding act of supernatural strength, and we will get them…

The Danger of Success

The more God blessed Samson, giving him strength to fight his foes, the more Samson grew confident of his own invulnerability; and the more he engaged in irresponsible behavior. In other words, Samson's heart used God's blessings as a reason to forget God.

As we saw in the Gideon cycle (page 96), while adversity is hard on us spiritually, success is even harder. One Puritan minister, John Flavel, summed it up: "Outward gains are ordinarily attended with inward losses;" while, conversely, "inward gains"—growth in humility, self-control, wisdom—are ordinarily attached to "outward losses" of our finances, careers or relationships failing.

We now can begin to see how sin and grace function on two completely opposed bases. In grace, God takes even our weaknesses and failures and uses them for us, but in sin, we take even his gifts and strengths and use them against him. Our sinful hearts will find ways to use even God's blessing to ruin our lives. Paul speaks of this in Romans 1 when in effect he says that the worst thing God can do to us is to give us our desires—success! The most successful people in the world tend to be the people that are the farthest from God.

Why? Just as Samson falsely inferred from God's blessing: *I can't be defeated, so I can live as I like*, so successful people falsely infer from God's blessing: *I got this because I was smart and savvy. I am self-sufficient!*

Why, Delilah? (and Why, Samson?)

"Some time later, he fell in love with a woman in the Valley of Sorek"—Philistine territory—"whose name was Delilah" (Judges **16:4**). The name "Delilah" sounds like "the night." In **verses 1-3**, "night" was mentioned four times—now, Samson is lying in "the night's" bed. And it will be his downfall.

The Philistine leaders approach Delilah and promise her money "if you can lure him into showing you the secret of his great strength"

> Samson is lying in "the night's" bed. And it will be his downfall.

(**v 5**). And "so Delilah said to him…" (**v 6**). What motivates Delilah to betray her lover? Two things. Greed is the obvious one; but there is more to it than that. The people who come to Delilah are "the rulers of the Philistines" (**v 5**). This is no longer some band or clan of Philistines who are trying to pay back Samson for some incident. These are the leaders of the whole Philistine nation, which means that now Samson is seen as a national menace. For Delilah, it means that if she could turn him over to them, she would be a national heroine. So the potential wealth, power, and influence being held out to her is very great. She would be set up for the rest of her life.

Her first question is ridiculously obvious! She simply asks him how he "can be tied up and subdued" (**v 6**). Surely Samson is at least suspicious—but he does not leave her. Instead, he lies to her, answering that being tied up with seven undried thongs would leave him "as weak as any other man" (**v 7**). So she ties him up (**v 8**), hides men in the room, shouts: "The Philistines are upon you"… and watches as he effortlessly snaps the thongs (**v 9**).

"Then Delilah said to Samson…" (**v 10**). This is an astonishing line—Samson is still there, listening to her! Why is he playing such a dangerous game? His motives are harder to discern than Delilah's, since the narrator gives us less direct information about them. First, we can guess that Samson was motivated by his overconfident love of danger. It is possible that he has become as hooked on danger as he is on women. It gives him a "high" to be in danger, because it has always meant glory for him. By **verse 9**, he cannot be in any doubt about what Delilah is up to.

But second, it is also possible that Samson is in the kind of "denial" that is typical in classic addiction-syndromes. He may have so needed Delilah's sexual favors and adoration that he was in denial about her motives. Twice, she complains that "you have made a fool of me" (**v 10, 13**), and twice he lies to her in response (**v 11, 13**). But when she says: "How can you say, 'I love you,' when you won't confide in me?" (**v 15)**, and repeats that complaint (**v 16**), he tells her "every-thing" (**v 17**). Why? Because it is a not-very-veiled threat to their rela-tionship: *If you **really** loved me, you'd confide in me. If you don't tell me this, then you prove that you don't love me—and that's the end of it!* It is only then that he tells her the truth. That is evidence that he could not bear to disappoint her even though she was leading him to ruin. This is typical of many destructive relationships.

Samson and Delilah are an extreme case of using one another rath-er than serving one another. They say to each other: *I am with you because I love you*, but they mean: *I am with you because you are so useful to me*. Doubtless there was a lot of passion and romance here—but it was all done out of a motive of self-enhancement, rather than self-giving for the growth of the other. Samson was using Delilah to get sexual love and (probably) the thrill of danger. She was using him to get fortune and fame. It is a pretty obvious taking instead of giving, on both sides.

> There was a lot of passion here—but it was all done for self-enhancement.

But there are far less obvious forms of this kind of approach to relationships. It is very normal for men to pass over great women who are not great-looking. It is very normal for women to pass over great men who do not have good careers. From the start, we look for people who are useful in building up our self-images and/or in getting the kind of lives we want.

Another less obvious form is the helper-syndrome. Often one person in a relationship is needy and constantly in trouble, and the other person is the counselor-rescuer. How the needy person uses the rescuer is obvious. What is less obvious is that the rescuer is using the needy person as well. He or she needs them to get a sense of worth and/or a sense of moral superiority. He/she needs to be needed.

C.S. Lewis is very helpful on this:

"Need-love cries … from our poverty; Gift-love longs to serve … Need-love says of a woman, 'I cannot live without her'; Gift-love longs to give her happiness."   (*The Four Loves,* page 21)

"You cannot love a fellow creature fully till you love God."

(*The Great Divorce,* page 100)

Lewis is simply saying that unless you have some experience of God's love that fulfills your deepest needs, you will tend to use other people to bolster yourself or prove yourself. Unless you have that relationship with God, even the most passionate *I love you*s will really mean *I need you to make myself feel as if I am worth something*.

Samson's inner life and motivations show this lack of God-love that should be a warning to us all. Without it, we will—we can only—do the same thing in relationships (though not, usually, so blatantly and spectacularly!).

His Strength Left Him

Delilah, now knowing the truth, sends for her paymasters (**v 18**). The sleeping Samson is shaved; "and his strength left him" (**v 19**). What follows in **verse 20** is strange. Samson knows that he has told Delilah the truth, and must know as he "awoke from his sleep" that his hair has gone. Yet he thinks: "I'll go out as before and shake myself free," because "he did not know that the Lord had left him." He assumed his strength would still be there, even though his hair had gone. And why not? Samson had been slowly breaking his Nazirite vow over a period of time. He had been breaking it by touching a dead body and by throwing a "feast" (14:10—which was literally "a drinking party").

The key phrase is "I'll go out as before" (**16:20**). We have seen that no matter how, or how often, he broke God's law, God had always given him strength. Why not now?

It is truly strange that Samson did not leave after telling Delilah the truth (**v 17**). Instead, he went "to sleep on her lap" (**v 19**). Why? Because he did not really believe that his hair or his Nazirite vow was the source of his strength. He had come to believe that his strength was simply his; that no matter what he did or how he lived he would not lose it. His self-deception was not just psychological, but theological.

> Samson had come to see his strength as a right, not a gift.

Samson was unable to see how dependent he was on God's grace. He had come to see his strength as an inalienable right, not a gift of God's mercy.

The Philistines thought Samson's strength was magical (so they believed his lies about fresh thongs, new ropes and braided hair). Magic power depends on external conditions and their *exact* manipulation. If a love potion requires three pinches of ground newt's-eye, then two pinches won't do. And when you get it "right," the magic just happens. Magic is a matter of following the steps to the letter, which pushes a supernatural "button," and the power comes automatically. In fact, Samson had the same magical view of his strength— except that he thought that the power came automatically, regardless of rules. The Philistines thought: *He must do something to keep himself strong.* Samson thought: *I don't have to do anything to keep myself strong.*

But God's power is different. It depends on internal conditions, on a heart-relationship. There is no divine power without discipleship. So

Jesus sent his disciples out with the power of the Holy Spirit (Acts 1:8). What is that power? The power of knowing that Jesus promised: "I am with you" (Matthew 28:20). To be "with" someone is a **Semitic** phrase for relationship. And so what mattered was not so much that Samson's hair had been cut, but that "the Lord had left him" (Judges **16:20**). We cannot know why God chose to leave Samson to his own strength (ie: weakness) at this point, when he had not when Samson began to forget his covenant, his relationship, with him. Perhaps a line was crossed when Delilah's love mattered more to Samson than God's. Perhaps it was simply time to reclaim Samson spiritually, by giving him weakness in adversity, rather than strength and power. Whichever, God's strength—which Samson had come to presume upon—is taken away.

God's power flows within a commitment to love and serve God. But it still depends on God. He can work in our lives even when we are not following the "rules"—though (as Samson discovered) we cannot presume that he will. Divine power is not acquired externally (through following rules, God's or others), nor can it be lost easily (when we fail to keep our promises to God). It is unpredictable in the sense that it does not rely on a particular technique. This is what neither the Philistines nor (tragically) God's own judge understood.

We may not think that we believe in magic. But it is very easy to do so, with a Christian veneer. Why do we think God will bless us? Sometimes we think that he just will—he has in the past, he will today. We become complacent. At other times we think that he will bless us *only* if we push the right buttons, follow the correct recipe. We study the Bible, we pray, we go to church, we live rightly, *in order that* we will be blessed and strengthened by God. We do it mechanically, rather than relationally. Instead, our Christian duties (like our spiritual strength) need to flow

> It is very easy to believe in magic, with a Christian veneer.

out of a relationship with God, rather than being an attempt to *get* that favor and blessing from him.

Questions for reflection

1. How could the outward gains in your life at present become inward losses? Are there any outward losses that the Lord is using to cause inward gains?

2. How, and from whom, have you enjoyed receiving gift-love? When is your love need-love, and how will you love God enough at those points to transform it into gift-love?

3. Why do you think God will bless you? How does that display itself in your attitude to obeying him in ways you naturally like; and in ways you naturally find hard?

PART TWO

"The Lᴏʀᴅ had left" Samson (**v 20**). Now he really is "as weak as any other man" (v 7, 11, 13, 17). So he's seized, blinded, and shackled (**v 21**). The man who had burned the Philistines' grain (15:4-5) is now reduced to grinding it (**16:21**). For the first time in the book of Judges, God's judge has been defeated.

Why Let His Hair Grow Back?

"But the hair on his head began to grow again after it had been shaved" (**v 22**). Of course it did—this is what hair does! So why record it?

The point is that the Philistines *let* his hair grow back. They could not have been such fools as to miss the fact that his hair was growing long again, so they must have concluded that, once shorn, Samson was no longer a Nazirite. And that is true. The Nazirite vow (Numbers 6:1-21) put the Nazirite in a state of "consecration" for a definite period. Once his head was shaved, the period of consecration was over (v 18). Since Samson's strength flowed out of his dedication to the Lord through his vows, it seems natural to conclude that his power is over.

But this confidence of his captors in letting his hair grow shows a shallow view of God. Samson's strength had come not from the vows he made, but from the God he made them to.

Michael Wilcock puts it like this:

"[The Philistines] knew nothing of the God who does the unexpected (Ehud), whose strength is made perfect in weakness (Gideon), and who never breaks his word. That God had said that Samson would be a Nazirite 'to the day of his death' (13:7). His abandonment of his servant could not but be temporary. The promise was bound to hold, however Samson might despise it. There is grace

> abounding to the chief of sinners. 'If we are faithless, he
> remains faithful—for he cannot deny himself' (2 Timothy
> 2:13)."   (*The Message of Judges,* page 148)

So we see a remarkable case of one of the themes of Judges—the "conditionality yet unconditionality" tension. The Philistines knew only "conditional" gods, gods who were subject to magic manipulation. The God of the Bible, however, is a God of grace, who is faithful to us even when we are unfaithful to him. He is not bound or limited by the terms of the Nazirite vow. Samson's hair growing back is not meant to make us think: *Ah, now he has his hair, he'll be strong again, because his strength relies on his hair*, but rather: *Ah, the Philistines think his strength has gone because his vow has been broken. They don't understand that God's work and power are not constrained by or contingent upon his servants' obedience!*

Yahweh v Dagon

After all, the true contest is not between Samson and the Philistines, but between Yahweh ("the Lord") and Dagon, the false god of the Philistines. Who is the stronger? Who should Israel serve? All along, God has been working to "confront the Philistines; for at that time they were ruling over Israel" (Judges 14:4); but this rule is about spiritual idolatry as much as physical oppression. God rescues his people most of all from their idolatry, rather than merely from their local enemies.

And yet it seems as though Dagon has won. "The rulers of the Philistines assembled" to proclaim the apparent truth that: "Our god has delivered Samson, our enemy, into our hands" (**16:23**). The setting is the temple of Dagon (as the mention of pillars in **verse 26** makes clear). The people celebrate and praise Dagon (**v 24**); God's failed rescuer is brought out to "entertain us" (**v 25**).

Samson, though, is not finished yet. He asks to be "put ... where I can feel the pillars that support the temple, so that I may lean against them" (**v 26**). Under the roof held up by these pillars are great crowds, including "the rulers of the Philistines" and the statue of their god; on the roof itself are 3,000 more people (**v 27**). The scene is set; and, for only the second recorded time in his life, Samson prays. Always before, he has assumed that he will be strong, and has used his strength to save himself (14:5-6, 19; 15:3-5, 13-17; 16:3, 8, 12, 14). Once, he assumed wrongly (16:20-21). Now, for the first time, blind and weak, he simply asks. "O Sovereign Lord, remember me. O God, please strengthen me just once more, and let me with one blow get revenge on the Philistines for my two eyes" (**v 28**).

This must be why Samson's strength returns. For perhaps the first time, he is exercising faith. Some commentators have argued that the request of **verse 28** is simply a vengeful one—and it is true that there is no mention here of rescuing Israel, only of revenge for Samson's eyes. But against this, first, there is a new-found humility here. Samson recognizes that the God of Israel is sovereign (adonai)—remember, he is

> For perhaps the first time, Samson is exercising faith.

standing in the temple of the god whose followers he has spent his adult life sleeping with). Further, Samson knows not only that God is his God (elohim), but also that he is the saving, covenantal, relational God of his people, Israel (Yahweh). This is a very different Samson to the one who presumed on "his" strength, and who demanded that God give him water without thanking him for his power (15:18).

And second, Hebrews 11:32-34 says that Samson was a man of faith, and surely this is the only place in the story where it could be said that Samson exercised faith! Most interesting is the reference in Hebrews 11:34: "[they] were made strong out of weakness" (ESV). This is a great insight. Samson had been humbled into the dust and had seen his weakness. Thus, this last request is a departure from his previous feats of strength. In Judges **16:28**, Samson first asks : "Remember me," which is a humble request for attention. He knows he is quite forgettable, and that God has every right to ignore him. Second, he asks: "Strengthen me just once more." Here (at last) is an acknowledgment of his dependence on God's grace. Samson's real temptation had been to believe that we are blessed by God because of something great and deserving in us—complacently to see what he had been given by grace as rightfully his, to use as he wished. That, rather than Delilah, was his real sin! It is so hard to remember that we do what we do only because of God's grace, and that God's grace is given so that we might do what is pleasing to him and in the service of his people.

Samson and Jesus

Samson—and we—cannot know as he reaches for the two central pillars and braces himself between them whether God will hear his prayer. His hair has grown back, but as we (and now Samson) know, his strength is not magic and automatic.

With one final prayer: "Let me die with the Philistines!" (**v 30**), Samson "pushed with all his might"—we hold our breath—"and down came the temple on the rulers and all the people in it. Thus he killed many more when he died than while he lived."

The most important moment of Samson's life is his death. The most faithful event of his life is the manner of his death. And the most triumphant episode of his life is his death, as he at last, and at the last, performs the role of beginning to rescue God's people that God had explained to his mother when his angel announced Samson's miraculous birth (13:5).

Samson's death is, in two crucial ways, very different from that of the Lord Jesus. First, Samson is in the temple of Dagon as a result of his own inability to live under God's rule and for his glory. His downfall is brought about by his disobedience. The Lord Jesus always lived for his Father's glory, and died because of others'—our—disobedience. Second, Samson's death achieved the limited role God had raised him up for—to "*begin* the deliverance of Israel (13:5). Jesus' death achieved deliverance "once for all," a final rescue (see 1 Peter 3:18; Hebrews 10:10).

But in so many ways, Samson's end is a picture, a shadow, of Jesus' death. Tracing it allows us to grasp more deeply what the cross is about, and to worship the One who died for us. First, both Samson and Jesus were betrayed by someone who had acted as a friend—Delilah, and Judas. (Judas was, of course, not as close to Jesus as Delilah to Samson—but the One he betrayed was far purer and more deserving of loyalty than Samson.) Both were handed over to the Gentile oppressors. Both were tortured and chained, and put on public display to be mocked. Both were asked to perform (though Jesus, unlike Samson, refused). Both died with arms outstretched.

And both appeared completely struck down by their enemies, yet both in their death crushed their enemy—Samson, the Philistines and Dagon; Jesus, the ultimate enemy, Satan. As Samson brought the temple crashing down around Dagon and his followers, the spiritual power and apparent triumph of Dagon was reversed. Samson brought permanent alienation between the cultures, so that Israel would become distinct, no longer unknowingly and inevitably under the Philistines' power.

> Both Samson and Jesus in their death crushed their enemy.

On the cross, Jesus brought the power of Satan to nothing, disarming him (Colossians 2:15). How did the cross achieve this? It took away the penalty for our idolatry—death—so that Satan could no longer successfully prosecute God's people. And it took away the power of sin in our lives, enabling the Spirit to live in us to break the lure of idols in our hearts. Samson prefigures Jesus' triumph, at the cost of his own death, over Satan. As Samson killed many as he died, so it took the death of Jesus to "kill" Satan—the unseen power of idolatry, and the power of death itself.

And both were saviors alone. Othniel and Ehud had rallied all of Israel to fight their oppressors (3:10, 27); Deborah and Barak took two tribes (4:10); Gideon had only 300. By Samson's time, sin had so devastated the people of God that no one (including, for almost all his life, Samson himself) was willing to give themselves to the liberation battle (15:9-13). In the same way as the Lord Jesus would, Samson's did his act of deliverance alone, unlooked for and unasked for.

> "God had shown that he could deliver Israel with an army of willing volunteers; he had also shown that he could save with as few as three hundred ... But when the Spirit of God came upon Samson, the Lord showed that he had no need for even three hundred. He could deliver by one."
>
> (Edmund Clowney, *The Unfolding Mystery*, page 137)

We have in Samson the pattern of the victorious defeat.

In short, we have in Samson, more than in any of the other judges, the pattern of "the victorious defeat." Rejected, beaten, chained, all alone, and finally dying under an avalanche of his enemies, Samson triumphed. God delivered his people through the victorious defeat of one savior. David Jackman writes:

> "[The Samson narrative] begins with a strong man who is revealed to be weak, but it ends with a weak man who is stronger than ever he was before." (*Judges, Ruth*, page 243)

It is the gospel! Jesus became weak to become strong. But there is, of course, one last, crucial difference between Samson and Christ. With Samson's burial, his rule was over (**16:31**). His story was finished. But with Jesus' burial, in many ways the story had only just begun. He rules beyond his grave, not just before it. The One who became weak to save will rule in strength and power eternally.

Becoming and continuing as a Christian is about the same pattern—becoming weak to become strong. Only those who admit they are unrighteous receive the righteousness of Christ. Only those who know their life and strength are theirs purely because of grace are not living in the grip of fear, boredom, and despondency. Only those who know their own weakness are able to know God-given inner strength; the strength which enables us to avoid the pitfalls of Samson's life: pride, lust, anger, vengefulness and complacency.

Questions for reflection

1. Where in your life do you need to rely on God's grace instead of your own strength? How would doing this change your actions and increase your joy?

2. How does the manner and achievement of Samson's death move you to appreciate and praise the Lord Jesus for his?

3. How are you feeling weak today? It is God's strength that matters—how will knowing that enable you to have peace and purity in your weakness?

12. MEN WITHOUT CHESTS

In some ways, the end of Samson is the end of the Judges story. He is the last judge, and his death appears to be the last chronological event in the book. We leave with a dead judge, and a very incomplete rescue.

But there are five more chapters at the end of Judges! These last chapters of Judges are a departure from the earlier narrative structure. The earlier passages give us a bird's-eye view of things, only saying that the people "did evil in the eyes of the LORD" (3:7, 12; 4:1; 6:1; 10:6; 13:1). These next chapters give us a ground-level, detailed view of what life was like in Israel during those times—the two episodes (chapters 17 – 18, and chapters 19 – 21) are a double appendix to the book, balancing the double introduction (1 v 1 – 2 v 5, and 2 v 6 – 3 v 6). The passages in between showed us how God rescued Israel, but here we are given two case studies of the kind of spiritual condition he rescued them *from*. That is why these final chapters barely mention the LORD. They are showing us what life was like when Israel was left to their own resources. This view of humanity without God is so bleak that these passages are almost never preached upon or even studied.

No Substance

Much of chapters 17 and 18 revolve around Micah, a man "from the hill country of Ephraim" (**17:1**). He had stolen 1,100 shekels of silver from his mother, but having heard her call down a curse on the robber, he confessed the theft (**v 2**) and returned the money (**v 3**). Micah is neither a very good, nor a very bad, person. If he were thoroughly evil, he would not have given the money back—but, of course, if he were a good person, he wouldn't have taken it! And what seems to have prompted him to return the money is that he "heard [his mother] utter a curse" (**v 2**), rather than feeling any pangs of conscience. We have here a person of very weak character, with no principles. He is hollow—a man without very much substance within.

In response, Micah's mother reverses the curse, asking for him to be blessed instead (**v 2**). She is very forgiving! But how quickly she pronounces restoration! She does not look or ask for real repentance, and so there is no full reconciliation. Without going through that painful process, there is for Micah no deterrence to such behavior in future; no challenge to examine his own heart and the reason why he took the money; no humbling acceptance of the need for grace and change. A condemning and punishing parent hurts a child; but so does an excusing one. Her parenting helps us understand why Micah is as he is.

An Image Problem

Micah's mother is very orthodox in invoking the LORD's name as the source of blessings (**v 2**). This family does not worship Dagon, the Baals, the Ashtoreths and so on. They are worshiping the LORD in name.

But... with the returned money, she gives it "to the LORD," for her son "to make a carved image and a cast idol" (**v 3**). She gives 200 shekels to a silversmith to make into "the image and the idol." This is startling; it shows a blatant disregard for the second commandment (Exodus 20:4-5; Deuteronomy 4:15-17), where God says no one should make an image of him. He must not be worshiped in a form created and shaped by man.

Why does he say this? Because any graven image or depiction of God would automatically reveal part of God's nature but conceal another part. For example, Aaron had made a golden calf in the wilderness. This was not another god, but a way to worship God. But while the calf could symbolize the power of God, it could not show his righteousness or love. Or, if you painted a picture of God and tried to worship it—would it show him smiling and loving, or awe-inspiring and majestic? It can't express the full range of God's glory, and thus your view of God will be distorted. So worshiping God with images reveals an inward spirit which does not want to submit to God as he is, but which wants to pick and choose attributes in order to create a God who is palatable to us.

Of course, this is the basis of an old Protestant-Catholic debate. Protestants have always complained that the use of statues or "icons" for worship (ie: gazing at pictures of God, Christ or the saints) by the Roman Catholic and Eastern Orthodox churches is a bad idea. That is because the depiction tends to "hijack" the emotions in just one direction, showing God in only one aspect of his being.

But this is not the *primary* problem. The real issue in worship-by-images is the desire to shape and revise God spiritually. In modern terms, it is a refusal to let God "be himself" in our lives. We filter out (consciously or unconsciously) things about God that our hearts can't accept. In some ways, this is the main sin of our time. How often have you heard someone say: *I don't believe in a God like that—I like to think of God as...*? That is worshiping God through the work of our own hands. And we can do this without fashioning a physical image.

> The real issue in worship-by-images is the desire to shape and revise God spiritually.

The most serious way we do this is by consciously, intellectually rejecting part of the scriptural revelation of God. We do this whenever we say: *We can no longer accept a God who does this... or who forbids this...* When we use the term "no longer," we wrap ourselves in the mantle of so-called progress.

In fact, what we are really saying is: *Our culture's distaste for this idea means we must drop it! We must have a God that fits our culture's sensibilities.* This means we, like Micah's family, are reshaping God to fit our society and hearts instead of letting God reshape our hearts and society.

Another way we do this is by simply psychologically ignoring or avoiding those aspects of God's revelation we don't like. For example, God is very strong on us giving our money away and not spending it lavishly on ourselves. But we can just avoid thinking out the implications of this for our own lives. Or we may know that God is very strong on forgiveness and grace, yet live a life in which we are very judgmental and unforgiving. We are then worshiping a God who is a taskmaster, not a shepherd.

A third way we do this is by **subjectivizing** all morality. For example, two professing Christians may be having sex with each other though they are not married. Why? Because they prayed (good) and then "felt peace about it" (irrelevant!). They ignore the objective commands about sex and marriage which God has given them in his word. This is what Micah's family has done. They follow God's law so far, but they then twist or add to it so that they can do what they like.

Why is this such a problem? Because it makes it impossible to have a truly *personal* relationship with God. In a personal relationship with a real person, the other one can contradict you and upset you—then you have to wrestle through it to deeper intimacy. But when we simply ignore (either intellectually or psychologically) the parts of God we don't like, it means we don't have a God that can ever contradict our deepest desires or say "no" to us. We never wrestle with him. We never let him make demands on us. We can end up worshiping a much more comfortable God, but also a non-existent one.

> We can end up worshiping a comfortable God, but also a non-existent one.

Keeping Something Back

It is startling that Micah's mother shows her gratitude to the LORD by breaking his second commandment! But she is also being dishonest. Having promised "my silver" (**17 v 3**), she only gives 200 shekels of it to the making of the idols, keeping 900 back (**v 4**). Micah's mother does not really put God first, or give him sovereignty over every part of her life. She hedges her bets—giving some of her wealth to God, but holding most back. It is easy to use a lot of God-language, claiming to have Jesus as Lord, but in reality only obey him in certain "sectors" of our lives, preserving other areas in which we live as we wish. Or, we obey him only partially in every sector, keeping back some of our money (as here) or time or emotions or relationships as an "insurance policy," in case God doesn't "deliver" as we would like.

This sometimes can be pure hypocrisy, as when a person conducts a secret extra-marital affair. But, more typically, we simply fail to think out the implications of the gospel for every area of life. In Galatians 2:14, Paul has to confront Peter (an **apostle**!) with the fact that he is still allowing racist feelings and prejudices to control him in some areas of his life. Many professing Christians are completely un-Christian in the way they conduct their work life. For instance, they may be as shady or as ruthless as everyone else in their business. It is more than possible to "solemnly consecrate" our whole lives to God on Sundays, but then really give him *only* our Sundays.

Homemade Religion

Micah takes the idols and puts them in a shrine in his home (Judges **17:5**). God had said that there was to be a central tabernacle or temple, set up around the glory-cloud—the majestic presence—of God (Exodus 25:1-9). When the glory-cloud moved, the tabernacle moved. That was the place where the sacrifices were made, where worship was conducted, where the high priest's "ephod" or breastplate was, where God answered people's questions (**see** page 98). God had not allowed the Israelites to worship anywhere they wanted, but Micah sets up his own sanctuary for worship at his convenience. Israel's religion has become one of personal preference.

Further, Micah makes his own son into a **priest**. Again, this contradicts the **Mosaic** revelation that only those of the tribe of Levi were to be priests. Micah and his mother, however, want to lift one of their own blood into the priesthood. After all, a shrine needs a priest! Later, they will find a Levite, and swap priests (Judges 17:7-12). But obedience to God's commands in how to approach and worship him had become an optional extra, not a central principle.

Fundamentally, the faith of God's people is a revealed faith. God reveals himself in his word— we do not discover him through our reason or experience. In short, God says: *Worship me as I am, not as you want me to be, and worship me as my heart directs, not as your heart suggests.* Micah's family shapes a God who is convenient to worship. They follow the laws they like and ignore the laws they don't.

> God reveals himself— we do not discover him.

This is what it looks like for a society to do whatever they see fit (**v 6**). It does not have to mean a conscious rejection of God. Nor does it require no longer calling on God, or ceasing religious activity. In fact, religious activity is spreading in chapter 17—a shrine in your own house looks very committed! But this is religion on Israel's terms, according to each person's personal preference. It is a religion that is not about God and his truth and will, but about me and my ideas and preferences. It is a religion which seeks to control and tame God, to remake him in an image we are comfortable with. It is an easy, or an exciting, religion—but it is not a religion which will bring blessing or rescue.

Questions for reflection

1. Is there anything in the way Micah and his mother treat each other that challenges your own attitude to your parent(s) or child(ren)?

2. Which parts of God's word would you most like to be different? Are you ignoring them, or wrestling through them?

3. How are you, or how could you be, in danger of holding back an area of your life from God? Are you experiencing real blessing in that area?

PART TWO

Now I Know...

In **verse 7**, we meet "a young Levite from Bethlehem in Judah." He has left his hometown (where he should have been serving the people as a priest) "in search of some other place to stay" (**v 8**). When he meets Micah (**v 9**), Micah sees an opportunity to make his home-made, do-it-yourself shrine more impressive. The Levite agrees to stay with him as his priest (**v 10-12**). Micah's shrine now outwardly con-forms more closely to the basic rules of divine worship set out in the Mosaic law—priests must be Levites—while all the time rejecting the central principle of that law—that worship must be conducted accord-ing to God's word, not human ideas.

Verse 13 shows the whole goal of Micah's (and his mother's) ef-forts: "Now I know that the LORD will be good to me, since this Levite has become my priest." The purpose of his religious efforts is to get access to God so that he can get God to do what he wants. The goal of true faith is to give God access to your heart so that he can get you to do what he wants. Religion's true purpose is to get God to serve you; gospel faith's purpose is to get your heart to serve him.

But why would we ever really want to let God rule our hearts, so that we serve him? We never will if we reduce him to a man-made im-age, or to a projection of ourselves in our minds, or to a nodding don-key who agrees with what we already thought. We would never be moved to serve a small god like that! But when we have gospel faith, we know the real God, who out of his great power and love sent his own Son to die in our place and give us his righteousness, and sent his Spirit into our hearts to change us into the peo-ple we were designed to be, enjoying his blessing. If we know *that* God, why would we *not* want to serve him? The tragedy of man-made religion is that it

> The tragedy of man-made religion is that it always reduces God.

always reduces God to someone to be controlled, rather than seeing God as the One who is in control and is worthy of real, whole-life worship. And reducing God leaves us worshiping a god who cannot help or save or bless—as Micah is about to discover.

Desperate Dan

The time of Micah is a time when "Israel had no king" (**18:1**). The writer does not complete the couplet he uses in 17:6 and 21:25—but the implication is that what follows will be the outworking of doing what is right in your own eyes. "And in those days [the days with no king] the tribe of Dan was seeking a place of their own" (**18:1**). Why are the Danites still homeless? Because, while all the other tribes had partly fulfilled God's command to fight courageously and drive the Canaanites out of their God-given inheritance (see page 20), Dan had failed in their military obligation, and were "confined to the hill country" (1:34). The Danites did not even get into their land, but were forced to live a semi-nomadic existence in the mountains. So now they are in search of land they can settle in to plant, grow and eat crops. The Danites are a picture of the weakest of those who call themselves God's people—they are conspicuous by their absence in the list of tribes of Israel who are in glory (Revelation 7:5-8).

And, as a tribe, the men of Dan are exactly like Micah. They suffer from the curse of restlessness and alienation because they have not obeyed God. They have an idolatrous view of God, and ignore his word—he has already told them where to live, but they stop at Micah's shrine (Judges **18:2-3**) and ask the Levite priest to ask God whether their scouting expedition to a completely different area will be successful (**v 5**—notice the Danites don't call him *Yahweh*). Assured by a pagan Levite working at an idolatrous shrine (**v 6**), they find a good land which they can take by their own strength, with no need to rely on God (**v 7-10**). The Danites, who refused to listen to or trust in the LORD, decide that their "God" has blessed them (**v 10**), and set out to take the land (**v 11-12**).

On their way, they pass Micah's house (**v 13**). What could be better than for them to take a religious shrine to their new home? They "know what to do" (**v 14**), and take all that makes Micah's shrine so "special" (**v 15-18**). The Levite challenges them, but they point out that it is "better that you serve a tribe and clan in Israel rather than just one man's household" (**v 19**). It is quite a promotion for a man who had once been a homeless wanderer! Gladly (**v 20**), he "went along with the people."

This is ministry motivated by self-promotion. The Levite really serves only himself. He serves whoever will pay him (**17:10-12**); tells people what they want to hear (**18:6**); and moves on to more impressive things (**v 19-20**). His decisions are driven entirely by self-interest. Yet each one takes him further from the LORD. He began as a Levite in the town of Bethlehem of Judah, the foremost tribe (and, of course, the town which was the center of God's plans for his people). He moved on to the hill country of Ephraim and an idolatrous shrine. He ends up in Laish, outside the land God had given to his people, working for a tribe who would not reach heaven. In his own life and his own terms, he has achieved dizzying heights, running the worship for an entire tribe of God's chosen people. Yet it is hollow worship, which knows only the god of self-promotion.

> This is hollow worship, which knows only the god of self-promotion.

What Else Do I Have?

It is worship just like Micah's. As the Danite soldiers move on toward the land they have decided to settle in, Micah and his neighbors catch up to them, ready to fight (**v 22-23**). Why? Because the Danites have taken everything Micah has. "You took the gods I made, and my priest, and went away. What else do I have?" (**v 24**). Everything Micah had could be taken away from him. And he had nothing else. He had built up his religious life—added to his shrine an idol, an ephod, even a Levite priest—and had looked to it for blessing (17:13). But all that he had trusted in had gone. And he could not get them back—those who took the basis of his blessing were "too strong for him ... [he] went back home" (**18:25-26**).

In the end, self-made religion will disappoint. Whatever we make into our god—money, power, relationships or even a reduced, man-made version of the biblical God—will not deliver. The person who makes career their god will eventually find their route to blessing blocked by someone who is "too strong"—too able, too well-connected, too "lucky"—for them. The person who makes their image their god will find time an enemy too strong for them to hang onto their youth and good looks. Ultimately, death removes all the false gods we look to for blessing. Micah was blessed in that he discovered the emptiness of his god before he died, when it was not too late.

It is a great reminder that everyone is a worshiper. The only question is, who or what is the thing we look to for ultimate meaning and purpose and blessing? What is the thing about which, if it were taken away from us, we would say: *You took my god. What else do I have? Where can I go in life now? I have nothing left.* There is only one God who will never be taken away from us. He is the One of whom we can say, with Peter: "To whom shall we go? You have the words of eternal life" (John 6:68).

When we find Jesus, we find blessing—but we only truly experience his blessing when we say to him: *Jesus, without you, what else do I have? You are my everything.*

We have to realise that there is nowhere else to go in life, and that there is no need to go elsewhere in life. If we know Jesus is ultimately all we have, we discover that he is eternally all we need.

> If we know Jesus is ultimately all we have, we discover that he is eternally all we need.

The Levite's Name

The Danites and their new priest continued their journey to Laish, "attacked them with the sword and burned down their city" (**Judges 18:27**). Rebuilding it, they "settled there" (**v 28**). Though they rename it Dan, it is really still called Laish, because it is not part of Dan's inheritance (**v 29**). This a tribe born into God's people Israel, but who now live outside God's land, do not listen to God's word, and worship him in a way entirely at odds with how he has commanded.

But there is one last, depressing twist to the story. Thus far, we have not been told the name of the Levite. But in Laish/Dan, the idols are set up for worship, "and Jonathan son of Gershom, the son [ie: descendant] of Moses, and his sons were priests for the tribe of Dan" (**v 30**). It is shocking to see that the Levite who will compromise on everything except his own interests is the descendant of *Moses*! It is proof that "God has no grandchildren"—every individual must find God personally and individually. No one is related to God by family tree; no tribe (or denomination, or local church) is related to him by pedigree. As scholar and writer Don Carson has said, one generation knows the gospel, the next assumes it, and the third loses it. Nowhere is this better seen in Scripture than in Moses' family.

> No one is related to God by family tree.

Jonathan and his sons will go on ministering idolatrously, worshiping the Lord in name but not in truth. Dan will be the site of idol-worship once the nation of Israel has split into two (1 Kings 12:26-30). But it will not go on forever. They will serve only "until the time of the captivity of the land" (Judges **18:30**, see 2 Kings 15:29). Just as they took the idols from Micah, so one day God will take the land from them.

What should Dan (and Micah) have done? Judges **18:31**: "all the time the house of God was in Shiloh." God has made it possible for people to approach him, worship him, know him and live with him.

The tabernacle, the place of God's presence among his people, was in Shiloh, and should have been the focal point of Micah and the Danites' lives. So should God's tabernacle today be for us—the man who is literally "the Word become flesh, tabernacled among us" (John 1:14). If we do not center our lives on Jesus as the way to approach, worship, know and live with God, we are centering our lives on man-made religion; on an idol; on something that cannot bless.

People Without Chests

These two chapters give us a great example of the **banality** of evil. Evil does not usually make people incredibly wicked and violent—that would be interesting, and tends to wake people up. Rather, sin tends to make us hollow—externally proper and even nice, but underneath everyone is scraping and clutching for power, in order to get ahead. We continually just step on each other, as Micah was stepped on by the Danites and his Levite. But after all, he had tried to rob his own mother before these men came and robbed him.

C.S. Lewis called these folk "men without chests" in *The Abolition of Man*. They may have reason (represented by the head) or visceral feelings and drives (represented by the gut), but they don't have hearts. They are not really choosing, but rather are being driven by their desires for power and gain, by their fears and anger. We are all in danger of being just as **banal** and hollow and uninteresting, if we insist on making God "tame" and banal! Only by worshiping the real God can we escape this boring fate and know the blessing of coming to the house of God, the Lord Jesus, the One who has the words of eternal life.

Questions for reflection

1. How will remembering who the real, powerful, loving God actually is shape your day?

2. Why is it wonderfully liberating to have Jesus as our "everything"? How will you enjoy him today?

3. What difference does having a gospel heart make to how you see and treat: your family; your boss and co-workers; your friends?

13. PEOPLE WITHOUT A KING

The first story in the ground-level appendix to Judges (chapters 17 – 18) was slightly comical, while also fairly tragic. Having read it, we are unprepared for and stunned by the violence in this second story, which is very dark and unremittingly tragic. It goes far beyond anything we have read already, even in the times of Abimelech and Jephthah. By modern standards, it is deeply repulsive—and it was by ancient Israelite standards too, going down in Israel's history as an episode of great shame (see Hosea 9:9; 10:9). Yet though it is very different in tone, its theme is the same—the desperate need for a Savior-King (Judges **21:25**).

Another Levite

The opening words: "In those days Israel had no king" (**19:1**) warn us, as we know from 18:1, that what will follow will be right in Israel's eyes, and evil in the LORD's. As in the first part of the appendix, a substantial part of the narrative revolves around a Levite (**19:1**).

But whereas in chapters 17 – 18 the Levite was concerned with self-promoting religious activity, this Levite is introduced as having a "concubine" (**19:1**)—a second-class wife, a sex-object (so the Levite is both the "husband," **v 3**, and the "master," **v 27**, of this woman). While God makes clear in Genesis 2:24 that marriage is to be between one man and one woman, many believers in subsequent times followed their society and had multiple wives and concubines (eg: Abraham, Genesis 16:2-3). But from Abraham through Jacob down to Solomon, the practice of **polygamy** always brought heartache and pain, without exception. It is a deeply ominous opening that this Levite, who was supposed to be set apart as holy, has instead been swept into pagan culture, taking a concubine. This Levite, we will see, is concerned with self-promoting relationships.

My Woman, My Property

The relationship between the man and his concubine is not a smooth one. Literally, she "plays the harlot" (Judges **19:2**)—commits adultery—and then leaves him and returns to her father's house (in Bethlehem, the town the Levite in chapters 17 – 18 had left). This is a total alienation, since to leave a master and a marriage (even though this one is a second-class one) was absolutely impermissible.

Yet the Levite waits four months before going to "persuade her to return" (**19:3**). Some have proposed that he was giving her time to "cool off"—but that is surely reading modern sensibilities back into the text. He evidently was not too bothered about having his concubine back, but eventually he either wanted the sex or the status (or both). These verses show us that this is neither a loving nor a lasting relationship.

The concubine's father "gladly welcomed him ... prevailed upon him to stay," and persuaded him to remain for five days (**v 3-8**). Ancient Near Eastern culture demanded that hospitality be shown, so in one sense the father's treatment of the Levite is only to be expected; yet these verses describe him as *over*-solicitous, almost desperate-sounding. Why? The penalties for both adultery and leaving an owner were severe—death, and disgrace for the family. The father appears to be ensuring that the Levite will not "press charges," and is deeply relieved that he has simply come to take her home again.

Interestingly, there is nothing in the text to say that the woman *was* persuaded. All the action shifts to the interaction between her father and her "husband." We are never told that she listened to the Levite or that she agreed to return. Every indication is that the father gave her back to the Levite, without her having any choice or making any decision. Both father and "husband" treat this woman as an object. One wants to avoid disgrace. The other wants to secure sexual favors. Neither care about the woman herself.

It is worth noting that, unlike every other section in Judges, none of the characters are named (apart from the priest, Phinehas, in 20:28). This anonymity is meant to suggest that these men and women stand for all of their "type" in Israel. This is how Levites lived. This is how fathers thought. This is how women were treated. It is a dark picture, which is about to become far darker.

Don't Do This Disgraceful Thing

After five days, in the afternoon, "the man, with his concubine ... got up to leave" (**19:9**). Despite the efforts of the concubine's father, they set off towards Jebus—a town which should be Benjamite but, because of their failure to obey God fully, remains Canaanite (1:21). Because the day is almost over as they reach Jebus, the Levite's servant suggests stopping there (**19:11**), but the Levite is unwilling to "go into an alien city, whose people are not Israelites" (**v 12**). Despite the Canaanization of Israel, clearly he is not confident that, as Israelites, they will be safe in Jebus. He decides to "try to reach Gibeah or Ramah" (**v 13**)—Benjamite, and therefore safer, places. As the "sun set," they reach "Gibeah in Benjamin," and stop to stay the night (**v 14-15**).

Immediately, we see that all is not well. They do not find anyone to speak to them or welcome them (**v 15**). The hospitality shown by the concubine's father is conspicuous by its absence. Only an old Ephraimite—not a Benjamite—speaks to them, and, hearing who they are and where they are going, welcomes them into his house (**v 16-21**). **Verse 20** hints that there is something more dangerous in this town than indifference: *Whatever you do*, he is saying, *don't spend the night in this square.* What is going on? This is not the wilderness! This is not a Canaanite town! This is Israel, God's land! What is so dangerous about the square?

Verse 22 shows us. "Some of the wicked men of the city … shouted to the old man … 'Bring out the man who came to your house so we can have sex with him'." Bravely, the owner goes outside and makes two points (**v 23**): first, that of itself this would be a "vile" action; further, that as "this man is my guest," to whom he has a duty to show hospitality and give protection, what they propose would be doubly "disgraceful."

But then he does something horrific: he offers them his own daughter and the Levite's concubine (**v 24**). In seeking to protect his house-guest, he offers two women up to rape. Why? Why does he not offer the Levite's man-servant (after all, it is a man who is being demanded by the gang)? Because the Ephraimite, like the Levite and the concubine's father, sees women as property, less valuable and more expendable than a man. This was the view of women held by the surrounding cultures (though, tragically, the concubine couldn't have been *less* safe in Canaanite Jebus); and this was the view imbibed by the men of Israel, rather than the creation principle of God, that man and woman are *both* created in his image, both equally intrinsically valuable.

> We should be very cautious of drawing neat lines between this incident and our own times.

This is such a terrible incident that we should be very cautious of drawing neat lines between it and our own times. But perhaps it is worth asking ourselves these questions, if we are Christian men: *Are there ways in which we listen to our culture about how we should view (either treat, or look at) women? In what ways are we in danger of treating women as property, as things?*

Israel's Sodom

What is happening here in Gibeah is very similar to the events in Sodom in Genesis 19:1-11. Strangers come to the town (angels, in

Genesis 19). Men surround the house, pound the door, and demand to have sex with a man/men. The host begs the men not to do this, and offers some women instead. The only differences are that in Sodom every man was part of the mob; here, it is "some of the wicked men." And in Sodom, the visitors were angels, who simply struck the men blind. In Gibeah, the Levite "took his concubine and sent her outside to them, and they raped her and abused her throughout the night" (Judges **19:25**). It is worth remembering that this really happened. We should feel repulsed and upset.

Sodom is the great Old Testament example of rebellion against God that rightly brings upon itself the judgment of God. The parallel between that pagan city and Israelite Gibeah carries an obvious message. Here are the people of God, who have been given the covenants of Abraham and Moses, the law and the prophets, the tabernacle, the exodus, and more recently the savior-judges. Yet despite all this, they are no better than the Canaanites and pagan nations who had received none of these blessings. God's people prove to be no better. They have become like Sodom.

There Was No Answer

These next verses are gut-wrenching in their brevity and poignancy. At dawn (after a whole night) the woman is set free (**v 25**). She returns to the house, and "fell down at the door and lay there" (**v 26**). The Levite finds her 'fallen in the doorway of the house, with her hands on the threshold" (**v 27**). When he speaks to her, "there was no answer" (**v 28**). The narrator's sparse account draws our hearts out towards her, because, as Arthur E. Cundall describes:

"If ever a human being endured a night of utter horror, it was
[she] … that night must have been for her … as dark as the pit
itself." (*Judges and Ruth*, pages 197-198)

The narrator gives us far more detail about the Levite. Having "sent [the woman] outside to them" (**v 25**), he then, almost unbelievably, went to bed and then "got up in the morning" (**v 27**). Rather than trying to find her, he made preparations to "continue on his way." Then, as she lay "fallen in the doorway of the house, with her hands on the threshold" (**v 27**), he simply told her to *Get up and get going!*, like someone would speak to an animal. And "when he reached home, he took a knife and cut up his concubine, limb by limb, into twelve parts and sent them into all the areas of Israel" (**v 29**). This is incomprehensible callousness and inhumanity, toward a woman who was his lover.

Why, when the Levite seemed so unconcerned about the brutal rape and subsequent death of his concubine, does he then send her body parts around Israel? Because he wants vengeance on the men of Gibeah—not for the treatment of the woman (after all, he sent her out to them), but for the loss of his property. There is deep irony in the reaction throughout Israel (**v 30**). They are right: "such a thing has never been seen or done" in Israel—but it is not only the Gibeonites' attitudes and actions, but the Levite's, which are reprehensible. The narrator makes quite clear that there is sin on all sides.

Editing Truth

Israel does not see this, however. "All the Israelites … came out as one man and assembled" (**20:1**). An army of 400,000 men gathers (**v 2**). Israel is united, for the first time since Othniel's judgeship. But it is united in its repugnance to something done by its own people, within its own borders; and it will listen not to God, nor to a judge, but to a deeply morally compromised Levite (**v 3**).

The Levite's account of what happened is remarkably self-serving, well edited to hide any wrongdoing on his part. Underlining where the atrocity happened (**v 4**), he claims "the men of Gibeah" (rather than the reality of "some of the wicked men," 19:22) were "intending to kill me" (**20:5**), when in fact they wanted to rape him (19:22). He omits to mention that he callously sacrificed his concubine rather than fighting to protect her, reporting only that "they raped" her (**20:5**). No one hearing this account would have suspected that he contributed to the death of the girl.

The point is that while the men of Gibeah are certainly villains, overtly and heinously sinful, the Levite's moral performance is, though more subtle, no better. This episode of history is enacted proof of the first two and a half chapters of Romans, where Paul says that the obviously debauched and godless pagan world is lost in sin, but then points out (Romans 2) that the moral, religious, externally "good" person is also lost in sin. Under the surface, they neither care about God, nor about others. He sums it up with the categorical statement: "There is no one righteous, not even one ... All have turned away, they have together become worthless" (Romans 3:10,12). No one in this story is righteous. No one in the world is.

How Do We React?

How should we react to the events recorded in Judges 19? We should mourn. These are God's people. They are our spiritual ancestors. And they show us, to an extent, ourselves. We may have secrets buried deep that bear resemblance in some (perhaps small) way to the conduct of the Gibeonites. Or we may not have committed such things, but (like the Levite) have failed to prevent them, enabling them through inaction. We will have all told ourselves and others a better story about ourselves and our conduct than the whole truth would reveal. And, as the book of Judges has repeatedly challenged us about, we will all

> We will all have told ourselves a better story about ourselves than the whole truth would reveal.

have allowed ourselves, unconsciously and even consciously, to be shaped and enslaved by our culture rather than by the LORD, whose name we call on, just like Israel.

Judges 19 should move us and prompt us to mourn, for them and for ourselves. "No one [is] righteous" because we live as though we have "no king" (19:1, 21:25). What we need is a King who will rescue us, rule us and change us. We can only appreciate the gospel—that in Jesus, this is who we have—if we first grasp that we are more wicked and more desperate than we ever imagined.

Questions for reflection

1. When do you find it easiest to edit the truth about your thoughts, words, or actions?

2. Are there well-buried secrets in your life which you need to confess, mourn and repent of, knowing that despite who we are, God is full of grace toward us?

3. What happens to our understanding of "the gospel" if we don't admit our own inherent sinfulness?

PART TWO

My People, My God

Israel is now united as at no time since chapter 3. They are "as one man" (**20:8, 11**), and commit to raising and supplying an army against the single town of Gibeah, to "give them what they deserve" (**v 9-10**). While the last judge, Samson, had to fight the Philistines single-handedly, Israel join together in determination to destroy their own.

But first, they send men to Benjamin, asking them to hand over the rapists, so that they can "purge the evil from Israel" (**v 12-13**). But this creates more problems than it solves. The Benjamites "would not listen" (**v 13**), and instead unite at Gibeah "to fight against the Israelites" (**v 14**), summoning 26,700 soldiers including some crack troops (**v 15-16**) to face the 400,000 Israelites (**v 17**).

Why does the tribe not just turn over the guilty men to face justice? One idol that is most destructive to human unity is the idol of our blood or kindred; the attitude of *my family/country, right or wrong*. Though common decency tells us that the men of Gibeah had violated all moral standards, the Benjamites close ranks and refuse to allow any outsiders to find fault with any insiders. When we put our blood or racial ties or community above the common good and the transcendent moral order, we make a god of "our own" people.

So now we see how sin builds upon itself. The callousness of the Levite and the sexual licentiousness of some local hooligans have turned into a full-blown civil war because of the lack of candor of the Levite master, and the pride of the Benjamites.

A Vindictive Massacre

There is great tragedy in **verse 18**. In the beginning of the book, as Israel began to settle Canaan, they had asked the LORD: "Who should be the first to go up and fight?" (1:1) for their inheritance, so that God's people could live in God's land and worship God within the sight of, but not intermarried with, other peoples. He had answered: "Judah" (v 2). Now they enquire of God (notably, his covenant name is used in 1:1, but not in **20:18**): "Who of us shall go first to fight?" Again, God replies "Judah." But they are not going to fight God's enemies, but God's people. The writer is showing that the failure to conquer Canaan and walk with God has led to civil war and **fratricide**.

> The failure to conquer Canaan and walk with God has led to civil war.

And that civil war begins in **verses 19-20**. The Benjamites live in the hills, which favored a defending force. So although vastly superior in numbers, the Israelites can only send in one or two tribes at a time to fight in the narrow space defended by the Benjamites on the first and second days (**v 20, 24**). Both times, the Benjamites defeat the rest of Israel (**v 21, 25**). And although on both days, God answers their questions about who to send and whether to fight (**v 18, 23**), these are no longer guarantees of success, as they were in the past (God is saying: *Go, but not I will go with you*).

This is a humbling experience for Israel. They were so convinced of the rightness of their cause that at first they did not ask God whether to fight, merely who should fight (**v 18**); and their question in **verse 23** does not really allow for an answer of *No*. Now, after their second reverse, they weep, fast, and sacrifice (**v 26**), and through the high priest humbly ask whether *or not* they should fight their brother Benjamites again (**v 27-28**). They are, for these few verses, living as Israel should. And "the Lord responded, 'Go, for tomorrow I will give them into your hands'" (**v 28**).

This time, Israel sets up an ambush (**v 29**), draws the main Benjamite force out of their stronghold (**v 30-33**) to give themselves space to attack in force (**v 34**); and God grants them victory (**v 35-36**). This happens as the men of the ambush "put the whole city [of Gibeah] to the sword" (**v 37**) while the fighting continues outside. So the

Benjamites think they are winning (**v 39**), but in fact they have lost (**v 40-41**). Israel turns on the Benjamite army, and soon all but 600 men of the tribe of Benjamin are destroyed (**v 42-47**). The victory is complete.

But the slaughter is not. Turning back, Israel "put all the towns to the sword" (**v 48**). Every single man, woman, child and even animal is slaughtered. This is not justice; it is genocide. Justice would at the very most demand the execution of the hooligans of Gibeah, and just possibly the Benjamites who came out to fight for them. What justification was there for the slaughter of the whole Benjamite society? This is the work of bitterness—which demands not one eye, but two, in revenge for every one eye lost.

The root of bitterness always flowers into vindictiveness. On a tribal or national level, it looks like Judges 20. On a personal level, it can seem less extreme. But the destructiveness is still real, though scaled down. And the only way to avoid bitterness is to practice forgiveness. Nothing else will uproot angry resentment.

How can we do this?

First, we have to realize *what* forgiveness is. Forgiveness is granted before it is felt (Luke 17:3-6). Forgiveness is primarily a promise to… not bring the wrong up with

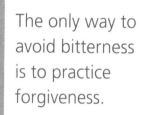

The only way to avoid bitterness is to practice forgiveness.

the person; not bring it up with others; and not bring it up in your own thoughts. It is a promise to not dwell on the hurt or nurse ill-will toward the other. These are under the control of your will. You are not able to keep a thought from occurring to you, but you don't have to entertain it.

Second, we have to realize *how* forgiveness is possible: only because you see and feel the reality of God's massive and costly forgiveness of us through Christ (Matthew 18:21-35). Only the knowledge of our debt to God can put into perspective someone else's debt to us. The forgiveness of Christ gives us the emotional humility to forgive (*Who am I to withhold forgiveness when I am such a sinner?*) and emotional resources to forgive (*What has this person really robbed me of, when I have so much in Christ?*).

If with our hearts we dwell on Christ's forgiveness of us, and with our wills we practice forgiveness of others, then slowly a feeling of forgiveness will come.

Lastly, we must forgive in our hearts even before we try to be reconciled to someone who has done wrong (Mark 11:25). That way we won't be too angry in our discussion with them and slip into trying to "score points" or to humiliate the person. In reconciliation we are trying to restore the relationship. We do that by admitting everything wrong we have done, by then pointing out any injustice that they have done, and then asking to be reconciled.

This is what no one had done—not the Levite, the Israelites, nor the Benjamites. The results have already been catastrophic, and they will get still worse.

The Problem of the Oath

"The men of Israel had taken an oath at Mizpah," when they gathered to hear from the Levite and pronounce judgment on Gibeah. It was a rash vow: "Not one of us will give his daughter in marriage to a Benjamite" (**21:1**). This created a huge problem for them. They had put all the Benjamite women to death, could not give the 600 surviving men their own daughters to marry, and so had effectively exterminated a whole tribe. As they complain to God (**v 3**), this means that "one tribe [will] be missing from Israel today."

It is incredible that they should "weep bitterly" about this to God (**v 2**), asking: "Why has this happened?" as though it is somehow God's fault. It was their rash oath, followed by their massacre of their brothers and sisters in Benjamin, which caused this. They should know exactly why this has happened! But it is easier for them to put God in the wrong than to engage in self-reflection.

And because there is no self-reflection, they do not learn from their mistake. As they build an altar and offer sacrifices (**v 4**), we discover that they had made

> It is easier to put God in the wrong than to engage in self-reflection.

another foolish oath—"that anyone who failed to assemble before the Lord at Mizpah should certainly be put to death (**v 5**).

So, having repeated the problem to each other (**v 6-7**), they discover that the men of Jabesh Gilead had "failed to assemble before the Lord at Mizpah" (**v 8-9**). This presents a potential solution. Since the men were not there, they have not promised not to give their daughters to the Benjamites in marriage. So, to keep their vow, the assembly dispatches a small army to the town (**v 10**), killing "every male and every woman who is not a virgin" (**v 11**) and carrying off the 400 virgins to marry Benjamites (**v 12-14**).

"But there were not enough" for all 600 remaining men of Benjamin. The people grieved "because [from their perspective] the Lord had made a gap in the tribes of Israel" (**v 15**). Again, they repeat the problem caused by their oath (**v 16-18**). Then, another solution presents itself. "There is the annual festival of the Lord" nearby (**v 19**), and they send the Benjamites off to "rush from the vineyards and each of you seize a wife from the girls of Shiloh" (**v 20-21**). The ingenuity of this is that, because these girls have been forcibly abducted, their fathers will not be oath-breakers, "since you did not give your daughters to them" (**v 22**).

"So that is what the Benjamites did" (**v 23**). An assembly which had gathered to do justice for a single raped and murdered woman ends up planning and promoting the murder of a whole town, and the abduction and rape of the girls of two Israelite towns. And everyone returns home (**v 24**)—apart from the unmarried women of Jabesh Gilead and Shiloh.

Solutions Causing Problems

Again, the narrator reminds us that these were people without a God-given king; a people who each "did as he saw fit" (**v 25**). All the way through the last two chapters, Israel has failed to look to the LORD for guidance. They ignore his word, and only enquire of him at the tabernacle *after* a decision of theirs goes wrong.

This is a functionally pagan culture. It takes decisions at best based on human reasoning, and at worst hastily and vengefully. Each step Israel takes is intended to "purge the evil" (**20:13**), and to solve the problem created by their previous actions; each, it turns out, causes even bigger problems. God is only a convenient person to take the blame for their mistakes.

This is the problem with human solutions to what is essentially a spiritual problem—the (humanly speaking) intractable problem of evil. There is no military campaign or state policy which can solve a problem which resides in and issues from the human heart. Only a revival of faith in God can do this. But Israel have never recognized that they are as much under oppression and slavery as if they had a foreign master. They are spiritually in darkness, *but they don't realize it.*

These chapters are a picture of how societies not centered on God must function: worshiping something other than the true God; deciding what seems right, logical and reasonable in their own eyes; wondering why things never seem to go much better; and then deciding that God, if he exists, cannot much care for people.

But of course, this is also a picture of the people of God—today, the church. No pagans were to blame for the oppression, rape, murder, massacre and abduction. It was *all* Israel's doing. All through the book of Judges, and nowhere more so than at its end, Israel's worst enemy was Israel. So often, sadly, the same is true of God's people today:

"No other book in the Old Testament offers the modern church as telling a mirror as this book. This book is a wake-up call for a church moribund in its own selfish pursuits. Instead of heeding the call of truly godly leaders and letting Jesus Christ be Lord

of the church, everywhere congregations and their leaders do
what is right in their own eyes."

(Daniel I. Block, *Judges-Ruth,* page 586)

We find it very easy to blame others for the weakness of the church.
We look at surrounding cultures which live so very differently from
us and call us to follow them. We wonder why God does not give
unity, or send revival. We look everywhere but at ourselves. But these
chapters of Judges force us to do just that.

The King We Need

But the whole book of Judges also shows us that though we are the
problem, we cannot be our own solution. We need to search for a
king, just as Israel did.

Many commentators believe that the author is an **apologist** for
King David's rule, and that he is trying promote the importance and
support of Davidic kingship. He is saying: *Look at the inadequacy of
human nature! We need more than these episodic, charismatic military chieftains—we need a permanent king.* It may or may not be true
that he is aiming to promote David, but he certainly makes a powerful case for the insufficiency of human nature! The book of Judges is
not a "book of virtues" or a series of "moral exemplars." The judges
are "heroes of *faith*" only (Hebrews 11:32-34)—their heroism lies
only in the way they trust God to work for, in and through them *despite* themselves, using them in his grace to rescue his equally flawed
people.

The author convinces us that we need a savior—but what kind?
God may be using the author of Judges to show us realities beyond his
conscious and deliberate intentions. He has shown us that we need
a deliverer—but by the end of the book we have come to wonder
whether a mere human king will be enough. The histories of 1 and
2 Kings and Chronicles follow a long line of human kings who lead
people at best not much closer to, and at worst away from, loving

obedience to God. By the end of those books, we know that we need someone beyond David himself.

By the end of Judges—especially in the life of Samson—we first realize that we need a deliverer who can come without being called for, since human beings are not really seeking God (Romans 3:11; 2 Timothy 2:13). We will not be able to choose him; he will have to choose us (John 15:16). Second, we come to realize that this deliverer will have to do it all himself, since we will not be able to contribute anything to our salvation (Ephesians 2:4-5; Titus 3:4-6). Third, we are even given the mysterious hint that this deliverer will himself save us through weakness, through a "victorious defeat"—through his death, not just his life (Philippians 2:1-11). Fourth, we need a king who can "purge" us of evil (Judges 20:13) in our hearts, not just in our society. Surely the author of Judges spoke more truly and wisely than he knew! We need a king, but a greater king with a greater deliverance than any human can be or perform.

It is the psalmist who truly sees all the way to the horizon: "Let the heavens rejoice, let the earth be glad; let the sea resound, and all that is in it; let the fields be jubilant, and everything in them. Then all the trees of the forest will sing for joy; they will sing before the LORD, for he comes, he comes to judge the earth. He will judge the world in righteousness and the peoples in his truth" (Psalm 96:11-13).

Here, the word "judge" is used in its original sense of "rule with justice." The psalmist realizes that when the true Judge and King returns, all nature (and human nature) will finally blossom and reach peace and fullness. Not until then.

> We must look to the greatest King—or we will serve a false one.

For now, we all search for a king—someone to rule us, someone to rescue us. There is only one man who provides what we are looking for. We must look to the greatest King, the ultimate Judge— or we will serve a false one.

Questions for reflection

1. How does the idea of the idol of "my family/people/tribe" resonate with and challenge you?

2. How does knowing Christ's forgiveness of you shape your treatment of others? Is there anyone you need to forgive, as you meditate on Christ's forgiveness?

3. If you had to sum up the message of the whole book of Judges in a few words, what would you say?

GLOSSARY

Abram: (also called Abraham) the ancestor of the nation of Israel, and the man who God made a binding agreement (covenant) with. God promised to make his family into a great nation, give them a land, and bring blessing to all nations through one of his descendants (Genesis 12:1-3).

Advocate: someone who pleads on behalf of someone else, defending them from a charge.

Anomaly: something that differs from the norm; a rarity, or one-off.

Altars: places for making sacrifices to a god.

Apostles: men appointed directly by the risen Christ to teach about him with authority.

Annunciation: when an angel announces a miraculous birth.

Apologist: a person who defends or justifies someone or something.

Assimilated: absorbed, completely integrated so that there is no difference.

Baby Boomer: the generation in the US and the UK born between 1946 and 1964.

Banal/Banality: boring, ordinary, completely unremarkable.

Book of the Law: the law God gave to Moses at Mount Sinai.

Canaan: an area on the eastern Mediterranean coast, to the north of Egypt and the south of Syria (in modern-day terms). This was the area God promised to give Abram's descendants (Genesis 12:6-9), so it is known as the "promised land."

Chasten: correct someone or some people in a humbling way.

Civil Rights movement: I am referring here to the Civil Rights movement in the US—organized efforts to abolish public and private acts of racial discrimination against African-Americans (and other ethnic-minority groups) between 1954 and 1968.

Concubine: essentially a slave-mistress; not a prostitute, but not a wife in the full sense, either.

Covenant: a binding agreement between two parties.

Crossing of the Jordan: the Jordan river was the eastern border of Canaan (though two-and-a-half Israelite tribes settled in land east of it). When Israel entered the land under Joshua's leadership, God parted the Jordan river for them to cross (Joshua 3 – 4).

Deacons: literally table-waiters; in the church, deacons are church members appointed to serve the church in practical ways.

Deities: gods.

Discerns: perceives, sees the truth.

Discipleship: following Jesus as Lord and trusting him as Savior.

Doctrines: statements of what is true about God.

Egypt: the country where God's people, Abraham's descendants, were in slavery (see Exodus 1).

Ethics/Ethical: a set of moral principles.

Exodus: literally "way out" or "departure;" the historical period when the people of Israel left slavery in Egypt and began to travel toward the promised land (ie: the events recounted, unsurprisingly, in the book of Exodus).

Fratricide: killing a brother (or brothers).

Functional: actual, real.

Garden of Eden: the flawless place God gave the first humans in which to live, enjoy his presence, and work for him (Genesis 2:8-17); also the scene of those humans deciding to rebel against God's rule, part of the judgment for which was being shut out of Eden (3:1-13, 23-24).

Gospel: The proclamation that the man Jesus was also God himself, come to serve us and to rule us as our King; that he died for sins; that he rose to rule and give new life; that he is reigning in heaven and will return to restore the world. The gospel is good news to be believed, not good advice to be followed.

Grace: undeserved, overflowing generosity.

High priest: the high priest was selected from among the priests (see Priest) to wear the ephod (see page 98) and perform special sacrifices on the Day of Atonement (see Leviticus 16). He alone was allowed, once a year, to enter the Most Holy Place in the tabernacle/temple— the place where God's glory was.

Holy: totally pure; set apart.

Idol/Idolatry: something other than the true God, which is served and worshiped as the source of blessing and security.

Impute: a giving or sharing of a quality (good or bad) to/with someone else, so that that quality is completely credited to them.

Inerrancy: the doctrine that every word of the Bible is true and without any fault or error.

Infallible: the doctrine that the Bible will not lead us astray in matters of faith and practice.

Inference: a conclusion drawn from a source or fact, which is based on reason but cannot be proved.

Joshua: leader of the people of Israel after Moses. One of only two people who were both rescued from slavery in Egypt and also set foot in the promised land of Canaan.

Joseph: The second-youngest son of Jacob, and the great-grandson of Abraham. He was the first of Abraham's family to live in Egypt; the rest of the family followed him there, and in subsequent generations were enslaved.

Justified: the status of being not guilty, not condemned, completely innocent.

Locust: a large grasshopper. Sometimes locusts gather in huge swarms, eating all the crops in their flightpath. In a wholly agricultural society, a plague of locusts is unstoppable and catastrophic.

Lord: most English-language Bibles translate the name by which God revealed himself to Moses (Exodus 3:13-14)—*Yahweh*, or *Jehovah*— as "Lord." Literally, it means "I am who I am" or "I will be who I will be."

Manipulate: say or do something in order to be able to control or influence a person or event.

Meditate: focused reflection on God's word.

Millstone: a very heavy circular stone used for grinding grain.

Mindset: a way of thinking or looking at the world.

Mores: customs and conventions of a society.

Mosaic: of, or from, Moses.

Moses: the man God chose to lead his people out of slavery in Egypt, and to the promised land. God then met him at Mount Sinai and through him gave Israel his law and instructions for how to worship. Because Moses did not fully trust God at all times during the journey (see Numbers 20:2-12), he died within sight of, but before setting foot in, the promised land.

New Jerusalem: in the revelation given to the apostle John by the Lord Jesus, the New Jerusalem is the perfect place on earth where all God's people will live eternally, enjoying his glorious presence and worshiping him, when he returns to make all things new (Revelation 21 – 22).

Nominal: in name only. A nominal Yankees fan would be one whose actions and emotions are rarely, if ever, shaped by the Yankees' results, and who never accepts a cost or sacrificial commitment to support the team.

Nullified: made invalid.

Ordination: the public calling of someone to pastoral, teaching leadership in a church.

Pagan(ism): a word used in the Bible to refer to non-Christians (eg: 1 Peter 2:12; 4:3-5). Pagan religion (generally speaking) refers to a belief system including many gods who are unpredictable, and whose favor or blessing or protection needs to be bought or earned through ritual or sacrifice.

Paradoxical: two true statements that seem to be contradictory, but aren't.

Polygamy: the practice of marrying more than one wife.

Pragmatic: an approach based on what appears to work, rather than value or moral-based considerations. Essentially, the end justifies the means.

Priest: the descendants of Aaron (Moses' brother), of the tribe of Levi, were chosen by God to be set apart to work as priests in the tabernacle. They represented the people to God, by performing sacrifices on their behalf, and represented God to the people, by teaching them the law.

Ransomed: someone (or some people) who is freed from slavery or captivity, through the payment of a price for their release.

Red Sea: the sea to the east of Egypt. As the Israelites left Egypt, it lay in their path, and they were trapped between it and the pursuing Egyptian chariot-army. So God miraculously parted the sea for his people to walk through, and closed the waters over the pursuing Egyptians (Exodus 14).

Repentance: literally, a military word meaning "about turn." Used to mean turning around to live the opposite way to previously.

Repudiating: rejecting something.

Sacrifices: in pagan religion, sacrifices were made to appease the anger and so win the favor of, or earn blessing from, a deity. Within Israel, sacrifices were a God-given way for the people to maintain their covenant relationship with the Lord. A sinner could not approach God without there being death—the lamb or bull died in the place of the sinner in order that they could continue in covenant relationship with God.

Semitic: a language group which includes both ancient Hebrew (which Israel spoke in the time of the judges) and Aramaic (which Jesus would have spoken).

Snares: animal traps.

Sovereign: to have supreme authority / be the supreme ruler.

Subjectivizing: making decisions based on feelings or opinions.

Theological: focusing on God's perspective and the truth about him.

Threshing: the process of separating grain from wheat.

Tribes of Israel: There were twelve tribes who made up Old Testament Israel. Each tribe was descended from the son of Jacob whom they were named after (see Genesis 49:1-28).

Trinity: the biblical doctrine that the one God is three Persons, distinct from one another, each fully God, of the same "essence" (or "God-ness"). We usually call these three Persons Father, Son and Holy Spirit.

Vindication: being cleared of suspicion and proved to have been right.

Walls of Jericho: a major city-stronghold in Canaan, it was the first fortified place to fall to Israel. God achieved victory for his people by causing the walls to fall down (Joshua 5:13 – 6:21).

Wrath: God's settled, deserved hatred of and anger at sin.

APPENDIX: The "Judges Cycle"

APPENDIX: The Details of each "Cycle" in

	3:7-11	3:12-30	3:31	4:1 – 5:31
Worshiped	Baals, Asherahs	Unspecified idols		Unspecified idols
Given over by God to	Cushan-Rishathaim of Aram Naharaim	Eglon of Moab	Philistines	Jabin/Sisera of Canaan
For a duration of	8 years	18 years		20 years
How bad?	Subjected	Took tribute		Cruelly oppressed; village life ceased
Does Israel cry out?	Yes	Yes		Yes
Interlude before rescue?	No	No		No
Judge	OTHNIEL	EHUD	SHAMGAR	DEBORAH/BARAK
Of tribe / clan	Judah	Benjamin		Ephraim/Naphtali
Supported by	Israel	Israel		Zebulun, Naphtali
Infighting within Israel?	No	No		No
Victory?	Yes	Yes		Yes
Peace?	Yes	Yes		Yes
Duration of judge's rule	40 years	80 years		40 years

the Book of Judges

6:1 – 8:32	8:34 – 10:5	10:6 – 12:7	12:8-15	13:1 – 16:31
Baal, Asherah	Baal-Berith	Baals, Ashtoreths, gods of five other nations		Unspecified idols
Midian	Abimelech	Philistines, Ammonites		Philistines
7 years	3 years	18 years		40 years
Had to live in caves; crops ravaged.		Crushed— great distress		Almost complete integration
Yes	No	Yes		No
Yes— prophet		Yes		No
GIDEON	**TOLA, JAIR**	**JEPHTHAH**	**IBZAN, ELON, ABDON**	**SAMSON**
Manasseh	Issachar / Gilead	Gilead	Judah / Zebulun / Ephraim	Dan
300 men		Gilead, Manasseh		No-one
Ephraimites complain; two towns unsupportive	Shechem destroyed	Ephraimites slaughtered		Judah seeks to arrest Samson
Yes		Yes		No
Yes, though with idol-worship		No		No
40 years	45 years (in total)	6 years	25 years (in total)	20 years

APPENDIX: Map of Israel in the Time of the Judges

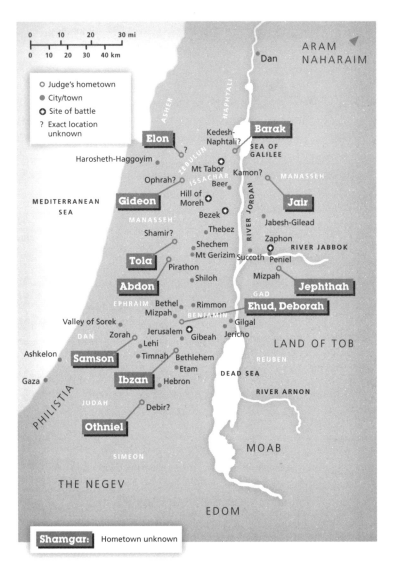

APPENDIX: The Issue of "Holy War"

The Problem

One of the biggest problems the modern reader has with Joshua and Judges in particular, and the Old Testament in general, is God's order to Israel that they "drive out" and evict the inhabitants of Canaan from their homeland. Here we have a nation doing what today would be condemned by world opinion. What is done seems identical to modern "ethnic cleansings," as when one ethnic group seeks to violently force out or wipe out another group. While we would consider it legitimate for people to engage in warfare in order to defend their homeland, most people today would not see it as legitimate to go to war to confiscate someone else's homeland.

And in addition, Judges seems to give a warrant for "holy war." If we allow the conquest of Canaan in God's name to be a righteous action, then why cannot others claim that they are going to war in God's name against "wicked infidels" and so treat them with violence.

What do we say to all this?

A False Solution

It is far too easy to respond that the Old Testament was a more primitive stage in religion, and that it contains many barbaric statements and directives that we cannot accept any more. There is a severe problem with such a view.

Why can't we accept them now? The main reason that we consider the conquest of Canaan problematic is because it breaks the sixth commandment ("You shall not murder," Exodus 20:13) and the eighth commandment ("You shall not steal," Exodus 20:15). But the Ten Commandments are in the Old Testament! So if we reject the Old Testament as God's true revelation, then on what basis do we object to the "immorality" of the conquest? It is arbitrary to say *I like Exodus 20* if we then also say *I don't like Judges 1*. If the Old Testament is not

God's word, then who's to say that one chapter is better than the other? To deny the authority of the Old Testament in order to "solve" this issue is like burning down your whole house in order to kill a rat that lives in it. If the Old Testament is not God's word, then we must find a totally different basis for what is right and wrong (which is impossible, see pages 124-125). But we can't quote the Ten Commandments anymore; so what is wrong with a little imperialism anyway?!

The real problem (and it is a real problem!) is that God allows the Israelites to do in Joshua and Judges what he forbids anyone else to do all through the rest of the Bible. The moral law, as it is laid down in both the Old Testament and the New Testament for all time, is completely against conquest. When we kill people who have not attacked us and take their land, that is always considered theft and murder. So why does God allow this exception here? And why can't this part of the Bible be used as a warrant for "holy wars" today?

A Way Through the Problem

There are several all-important differences which distinguish the mission of Israel to occupy Canaan from any other military action, either before or since.

1. The war is not carried out on the basis of race. God's order to evict the Canaanites is not a directive to remove or kill people of a different race. When the invasion of Canaan began, Israel's spies were helped by Rahab, a resident of Jericho (see Joshua 2; 6:20-25). Rahab was not only a Canaanite, but a prostitute—she could have been seen as both a racial and a moral "outsider." Yet because she trusted in the LORD, the God of Israel, she became part of the people of Israel and stayed in Canaan. The purpose of the mission was to "break down [the] altars" of the idols (Judges 2:2) and evict pagan worship (and therefore pagan worshippers), not necessarily the people of any particular race. So this campaign is not a warrant for the warfare of one ethnic group against another.

2. The war is not carried out on the basis of imperialistic expansion. Even within this special mandate, <u>God does not allow the Israelites to plunder or enslave any of the people with whom they do battle</u>. They are to be defeated and driven out—period. For example, in Joshua 7, Achan is judged for keeping plunder from a Canaanite town. What was normal for all military actions and invasions at that time was completely forbidden to the Israelites. Why? Because the purpose of the mission was not to become prosperous and powerful, but rather, to create a country in which the Israelites could serve and honor God.

    The need to evict the Canaanites was probably due to the Israelites' weakness in the face of temptation. In other words, the eviction was not a testimony to how virtuous the people were, but to how spiritually weak they were. This campaign cannot be a warrant for the imperialistic colonization by one country of another country.

3. The war is carried out as God's judgment, and through direct revelation. To Joshua (Joshua 1:1-9) and through Joshua (in Joshua 23:1-16), and again through the priest's ephod (Judges 1:1), God gives specific, verbal revelation to the Israelites to evict the Canaanites. Nothing less direct and unmistakable could be the basis for such action. It would not be enough to say: *We've thought about it and prayed about it and talked about it, and we think the Lord is leading us to break the sixth and eighth commandments* (or any of the other ones).

But why would God command such a thing? One theologian, Meredith G. Kline, has called this "the intrusion ethic." God, of course, knows the end from the beginning. He alone has the right and the knowledge to see persons who will be condemned on Judgment Day when his Son returns, and to bring a judgment down on those people "early." Thus God, the Judge of all, can determine to begin to mete out justice on them now, rather than waiting for the Last Day. Therefore, the future judgment "intrudes" on the present. This is not totally unusual, because the blessings of the gospel are also intrusions of the future grace into the present.

Therefore, this is not a mandate for believers in general to move coercively against unbelievers, nor any warrant for a "holy war" by one faith against another. The way we know the Lord's will is to read the Ten Commandments and the other directives of the Bible to us—not to try to imitate everything described in all the histories of the Bible. Many people run into the same problem when they say: *We are running our church just as God commands us to in the book of Acts.* In Ephesians and 1 Timothy, Paul clearly lays down principles for church order, which we don't always see in Acts. That's because at some points, the book of Acts only describes what the church did, not what God told it (and tells us, through his word) to do. We must be much more cautious in drawing hard-and-fast conclusions from historical passages.

What is the Bible?

This issue highlights the importance of the orthodox Christian view of God's revelation. All branches of the institutional church—Eastern Orthodox, Roman Catholic, and Protestant—historically agree that the Bible is entirely the revelation of God's will. There are two opposite views, however, that could be very dangerous and lead us into "holy war." On the one hand, some people believe that they are getting direct revelation from God—on an equal level with that which Moses or Joshua or the apostles received. If you believe in that sort of "continuing revelation," then there is no control or check against "holy war." You could always say that God is calling you to attack in his name and wipe out some group which is "of the devil."

On the other hand, many, many people do not believe the Bible is a divine and inerrant revelation at all. But if you don't believe in the authoritative word of God, then there is also no control or check against "holy war." You could always say that your conscience and conviction or culture is calling you to attack and wipe out some group of people.

But if I believe the orthodox view of the Bible, then there is a very real control and check on how I use political power. I know that God has spoken without error, in the Scriptures, and I seek to live in obedience to them; I neither add to his word, nor subtract from it.

Read With Humility

It is extremely easy for contemporary people to feel condescending toward, or offended by, the actions of many of those whose stories are related in the book of Judges. God's command to conquer Canaan is difficult enough to understand. But in addition, Judges recounts supposed "good guys" treating women, children and people of other races in evil ways.

But let's not assume that, if we had been born in this ancient era, we would have been so much more enlightened than everyone else. We should realize that we have the advantage of living in a society deeply influenced by the Ten Commandments and other biblical influences on our civilization.

So, when we read of these ancient men and women, we do need humbly to remember that our own inner natures and hearts are not fundamentally better than theirs were. Their flaws may be different, and their effects at times writ larger than ours, but they flow from the same rebellious hearts as ours. We must be willing to look for the ways in which we are like the people in the narrative, and not pander to our pride by focusing on the ways in which we are unlike, and "better than," them.

BIBLIOGRAPHY

■ Daniel I. Block, *The New American Commentary: Volume 6—Judges-Ruth* (Holman Reference, 1999)

■ Edmund P. Clowney, *The Unfolding Mystery: Discovering Christ in the Old Testament* (P&R Publishing, 1989)

■ Arthur C. Cundall and Leon L. Morris, *Judges and Ruth* in the Tyndale Old Testament Commentaries series (IVP Academic, 2008)

■ David Jackman, *Judges, Ruth* in the Mastering the Old Testament series (Word Books, 1993)

■ C.S. Lewis, *The Abolition of Man: How Education Develops Man's Sense of Morality* (MacMillan, 1976)

■ C.S. Lewis, *The Four Loves* (Houghton Mifflin Harcourt, reissued 1991)

■ C.S. Lewis, *The Great Divorce* (Harper One, reissued 2009)

■ Rebecca Manley Pippert, *Out of the Saltshaker and into the World: Evangelism as a Way of Life* (IVP, 1999)

■ Michael Wilcock, *The Message of Judges* in The Bible Speaks Today series (IVP, 1992)

Judges for...
Bible-study Groups

Timothy Keller's **Good Book Guide** to Judges is the companion to this resource, helping groups of Christians to explore, discuss and apply the book together. Six studies, each including *investigate*, *apply*, *getting personal*, *pray* and *explore more* sections, take you through the whole of Judges. Each Good Book Guide includes a concise Leader's Guide at the back.

Find out more at:
www.thegoodbook.com/good-book-guides

Daily Devotionals

Explore daily devotional helps you open up the Scriptures, and will encourage and equip you in your walk with God. Available as a quarterly booklet, the studies can also be accessed via the *Explore* app, where you can download Dr Keller's notes on Judges and other books of the Bible alongside contributions from trusted Bible teachers including Mark Dever, Al Mohler, Sam Allberry, Tim Chester, and Richard Coekin.

Find out more at:
www.thegoodbook.com/explore

God's Word For You Series

Find out more about these resources at:

www.thegoodbook.com/for-you

1 Samuel For You *Tim Chester*

"1 Samuel leaves us looking beyond it. The history of the first christs leaves us longing for the rule of the ultimate Christ. As we read this book, we see Christ Jesus with fresh colour and texture. And we see what it means for his people to follow him as King in an age that worships personal freedom."

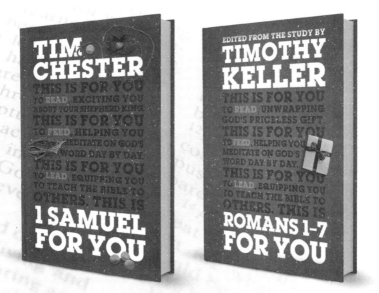

Romans 1-7 For You *Timothy Keller*

"Reading Romans, we should be prepared to have our hearts shaped and lives changed by God's gift of righteousness. It will prompt us to ask: *Have I, as Martin Luther put it, 'broken through' into the freedom and release the gospel brings me, both in terms of my future and right now?*"

Good Book Guides
for groups and individuals

Ezekiel: The God of Glory

Tim Chester
Pastor at Grace Church, Boroughbridge,
Yorkshire, UK

"Then they will know that I am the LORD"
is the repeated message of Ezekiel. In a
world of false hopes that will ultimately
fail, this is a message for everyone.

Daniel: Staying strong in a hostile world

David Helm
Lead Pastor, Holy Trinity Church, Chicago

The first half of Daniel is well known and
much loved. The second is little read and less
understood! David Helm leads groups through
the whole book, showing how the truths
about God in the second half enabled Daniel
and his friends—and will inspire us—to live
faithful, courageous lives.

Esther: Royal rescue

Jane McNabb
Chair of the London Women's Convention

The experience of God's people in Esther's day
helps us in those moments when we question
God's sovereignty, his love, or his faithfulness.
Their story reveals that despite appearances,
God is in control, and he answers his people's
prayers—often in most unexpected ways.

1 Corinthians 1–9: Challenging church

Mark Dever
Senior Pastor of Capitol Hill Baptist Church in Washington DC and President of 9Marks Ministries

The church in Corinth was full of life, and just as full of problems. As you read how Paul challenges these Christians, you'll see how you can contribute to your own church becoming truly shaped by the gospel.
Also by Mark Dever: 1 Corinthians 10–16

James: Genuine faith

Sam Allberry
Associate Minister, St Mary's Maidenhead, UK

Many Christians long for a deeper, more whole-hearted Christian life. But what does that look like? This deeply practical letter was written to show us, and will reveal how to experience joy in hardships, patience in suffering and whole-heartedness in how you speak, act and pray.
Also by Sam Allberry: Man of God; Biblical Manhood

1 Peter: Living well on the way home

Juan Sanchez
Preaching Pastor, High Pointe Baptist Church, Austin, Texas

The Christian life, lived well, is not easy—because we don't belong in this world. Learn from Peter how to journey on rather than retreat, and to do so with joy and hope, rather than gritted teeth.

thegoodbook
COMPANY

BIBLICAL | RELEVANT | ACCESSIBLE

At The Good Book Company, we are dedicated to helping Christians and local churches grow. We believe that God's growth process always starts with hearing clearly what he has said to us through his timeless word—the Bible.

Ever since we opened our doors in 1991, we have been striving to produce Bible-based resources that bring glory to God. We have grown to become an international provider of user-friendly resources to the Christian community, with believers of all backgrounds and denominations using our books, Bible studies, devotionals, evangelistic resources, and DVD-based courses.

We want to equip ordinary Christians to live for Christ day by day, and churches to grow in their knowledge of God, their love for one another, and the effectiveness of their outreach.

Call us for a discussion of your needs or visit one of our local websites for more information on the resources and services we provide.

Your friends at The Good Book Company

thegoodbook.com | thegoodbook.co.uk
thegoodbook.com.au | thegoodbook.co.nz
thegoodbook.co.in